to All Y'ALL!

The Sawyers

12/25/08

Colorful Cuisine

Fine Art and Cooking in Brentwood

This cookbook is a collection of favorite recipes,
which are not necessarily original recipes.

Colorful Cuisine
Fine Art and Cooking in Brentwood

Copyright 2001

Brentwood Academy Parent Association
219 Granny White Pike
Brentwood, TN 37027
615-373-0611

LC Control Number: 2001 129035
ISBN: 0-9709593-0-3

Edited, Designed and Manufactured by
Favorite Recipes® Press
an imprint of

FRP

P.O. Box 305142
Nashville, Tennessee 37230
1-800-358-0560

Art Director: Steve Newman
Book Design: Jim Scott
Project Manager: Ginger Dawson

Manufactured in the United States of America
First Printing: 2001

Cover Artist:

*Jennifer Padgett is a Nashville, Tennessee-based artist whose oil paintings show a harmony of
a moment and a mood. She believes painting is the artistic means of seeking truth. Her works
are characterized by a strong sense of light and color, and reflect her desire to share a candid
moment with the viewer. She studied painting at David Lipscomb University and developed
her style under the guidance of Dawn Whitelaw. Her works are included in collections
at David Lipscomb and Vanderbilt universities. Cover painting: Red Café.*

Acknowledgements

Thank you to the Brentwood Academy parents, alumni,
friends, faculty, and students who contributed to the
cookbook project. We also express our gratitude to
the Fine Art in Brentwood chairmen for their help in
making the concept for the book a reality. We appreciate
the support and expertise of FRP and Southwestern/Great
American. Thank you to Vaughan Printing Company,
and to Anna Pace for her legal assistance.

Mission Statement

Brentwood Academy is a co-educational, independent, college preparatory school dedicated to nurturing and challenging the whole person— body, mind, and spirit—to the glory of God.

BRENTWOOD ACADEMY

Contents

Brentwood Academy 6

Fine Art in Brentwood 8

Entertaining 9

Appetizers 27

Brunch & Beverages 45

Soups & Salads 71

Vegetables & Side Dishes 89

Entrées 107

Breads 141

Desserts 159

Cookbook Committee 185

Contributors List 185

Index 188

Order Information 192

Brentwood Academy

Founded in 1969, Brentwood Academy is an independent, co-educational day school serving just over 600 students in grades six through 12 through a unique "Triangle Philosophy" of education, which nurtures and challenges students in mind, body, and spirit to the glory of God.

Located on a 50-acre campus in the heart of Brentwood, Tennessee, the school is known for its fine academic and athletic programs. Brentwood Academy graduates have attended selective colleges and universities throughout the country and in several foreign countries.

A low faculty-student ratio of 1:12 allows for an exceptional teaching environment and over 75 percent of the faculty hold master's or higher graduate degrees. The entire campus is computer-networked with over 200 computers as part of the technological system.

A comprehensive Fine Arts program offers courses and extracurricular opportunities in studio art, photography, choral and instrumental music, drama, and forensics.

Spiritual Life offerings include student retreats, Bible studies, and service projects within the Brentwood, Franklin, and Nashville communities as well as in other parts of the country.

In the athletic arena, Brentwood Academy offers students team sports in football, basketball, soccer, softball, volleyball, track, cross-country, tennis, golf, and bowling. Additionally, physical education is offered and all students take part in physical activity each day.

Founding Headmaster William B. Brown, Jr., had a vision that Brentwood Academy would educate the whole person through a curriculum which enhances the students' educational experience academically, athletically, and spiritually. Today, under the leadership of Headmaster Curt Masters, Brentwood Academy continues to daily live out that early vision.

Fine Art in Brentwood

Since 1996, Brentwood Academy has presented an annual show and sale of fine art by artists from across the Southeast and around the country.

Fine Art in Brentwood, held the first weekend in December at the school, has been an overwhelming success since its start, and has provided significant support for programs and special projects at Brentwood Academy.

Featuring paintings by more than 50 artists, the event is a much-anticipated showcase for the arts in the Brentwood community. The prices of the artwork range from under $100 to several thousand dollars. All purchases are 30 percent tax deductible.

All of the artists who contributed paintings for Colorful Cuisine have participated in the Fine Art in Brentwood show.

Entertaining

Joanna Reed Caldwell

Joanna Reed Caldwell, who signs her works as Joanna, paints in her Coldwater, Tennessee, studio, using warm, glowing colors and selecting universal subjects. She believes the purpose of her work is to "make people smile, or maybe move one's soul." She said she strives to add a "touch of cheer and humor to our everyday lifestyle." Recent acrylic paintings feature whimsical French and Italian waiters.

Shown on overleaf: *The Art of Cooking*

Fine Art in Brentwood Opening Night

Caviar Artichokes

Baked Brie with Cranberry Chutney

Bread Bowl Dip

Curry Dip

Superb and Simple Chocolate Mousse

It's opening night for *Fine Art in Brentwood*, and artists and patrons alike are full of anticipation. In keeping with the elegant setting, a palette of gourmet dishes has been prepared for art lovers attending the first evening of the annual show. Striking decorations, classical music performed by student musicians, and superb food set the stage for a stroll through the aisles of exquisite paintings offered by talented artists.

Caviar Artichokes

2 (8½-ounce) cans artichoke hearts,
    drained
8 ounces cream cheese, softened
2 tablespoons sour cream

1 to 2 tablespoons mayonnaise
½ cup finely chopped onion
2 (2-ounce) jars black or red caviar,
    rinsed, drained

Chop the artichokes into very small pieces; drain. Mound the artichokes in the center of a serving platter. Combine the cream cheese, sour cream, mayonnaise and onion in a small bowl and mix well. Spread the cream cheese mixture carefully over the artichokes. Sprinkle the caviar over the top. Garnish with fresh parsley. Serve with butter crackers.
Yield: 8 to 10 servings.

Baked Brie with Cranberry Chutney

2 cups fresh cranberries
2 cups sugar
3 tablespoons water
1 Granny Smith apple, chopped
2 ribs celery, chopped
1 cup fresh orange juice

1 tablespoon orange zest
1 cup golden raisins
½ teaspoon ginger
¼ teaspoon cloves
1 (8-ounce) round Brie cheese

Combine the cranberries, sugar and water in a medium saucepan. Cook over medium heat for 5 minutes. Add the apple, celery, orange juice, orange zest, raisins, ginger and cloves. Cook for 35 minutes, stirring occasionally. Remove from the heat. Spoon ⅓ cup of the chutney on top of the Brie. Microwave for 1 minute before serving. Serve on a platter with assorted crackers. You may store the chutney in the refrigerator for up to 3 weeks. This chutney is also excellent served with chicken or pork.
Yield: 6 to 8 servings.

Bread Bowl Dip

1 (10-ounce) package frozen chopped spinach,
thawed, drained
1 (8-ounce) can water chestnuts, drained, chopped
2 green onions, chopped
1 cup mayonnaise
1 cup sour cream
1 envelope Knorr spring vegetable soup mix
1 round bread loaf

Combine the spinach, water chestnuts, green onions, mayonnaise, sour cream and soup mix in a bowl and mix well. Hollow out the bread loaf to make a bowl; reserving the bread. Spoon the prepared dip into the bread bowl. Cut the reserved bread into squares to serve on a platter with the dip. *Yield: 10 to 12 servings.*

Curry Dip

16 ounces cream cheese, softened
1/4 cup chopped peanuts
1/4 cup chopped green onions
1/4 cup bacon bits
1/4 cup golden raisins
1/2 cup flaked coconut
1/2 cup mango chutney

Combine the cream cheese, peanuts, green onions, bacon bits and raisins in a bowl and mix well. Shape into a ball and place on a serving plate. Top with the coconut and spoon the chutney around the ball. Serve with gingersnaps. *Yield: 8 to 10 servings.*

Superb and Simple Chocolate Mousse

1 cup (6 ounces) semisweet chocolate chips
2 eggs
3 tablespoons hot strong coffee
1 tablespoon orange extract
3/4 cup scalded milk

Combine the chocolate chips, eggs, coffee, orange extract and milk in a blender or food processor container. Process for 1 to 2 minutes or until smooth. Pour into 4 dessert glasses. Chill, covered, for 4 hours before serving. Garnish with mandarin orange sections. *Yield: 4 servings.*

Holiday Dinner

Rustic Corn Dressing

Roast Turkey with Maple Herb Butter

Baked Butternut Squash

Cranberry Salad

Pumpkin Chiffon Pie

Wassail Punch

Rustic Corn Dressing

1 (29-ounce) can whole kernel corn,
   drained
1 pound smoked bacon
2 cups chopped onions
1 1/2 cups chopped celery
4 garlic cloves, minced
1/2 cup (1 stick) butter, melted

6 cups Pepperidge Farm country-style
   stuffing mix
1 1/2 cups chopped pecans, toasted
1 egg, lightly beaten
2 to 2 3/4 cups chicken or turkey broth
1 teaspoon freshly ground pepper
1/2 teaspoon salt

Press the corn between paper towels to remove any excess moisture; set aside. Cook the bacon in a large skillet over medium heat until crisp. Remove the bacon from the skillet; reserving 2 tablespoons drippings in the skillet. Crumble the bacon; set aside. Add the corn to the skillet, tossing to coat with the drippings. Cook over high heat, stirring constantly until the corn is lightly browned. Spoon into a large bowl. Cook the onions, celery and garlic in the butter in a large skillet over medium heat, stirring constantly until tender. Spoon into the bowl with the corn. Stir in the stuffing mix, crumbled bacon and pecans. Add the egg, chicken broth, pepper and salt and stir gently. Spoon into a lightly greased 9×13-inch dish. Bake at 325 degrees for 1 hour or until brown. This dressing may also be used to stuff a turkey. *Yield: 10 servings.*

Roast Turkey with Maple Herb Butter

Maple Herb Butter
2 cups apple cider
1/3 cup pure maple syrup
2 tablespoons chopped fresh marjoram
2 tablespoons chopped fresh thyme
1 1/2 teaspoons grated lemon zest
3/4 cup (1 1/2 sticks) butter, softened
Salt to taste
Pepper to taste

Turkey
1 (14-pound) turkey, neck and giblets
   reserved
2 cups chopped onions
1 1/2 cups chopped celery, with the
   leaves
1 cup coarsely chopped carrot
2 cups low-sodium chicken broth

For the butter, combine the apple cider and maple syrup in a heavy saucepan over medium-high heat. Bring to a boil and cook for 20 minutes or until reduced to about 1/2 cup. Remove from the heat. Add 1 1/2 teaspoons marjoram, 1 1/2 teaspoons thyme, lemon zest and butter. Whisk until the butter is melted. Season with the salt and pepper. Chill, covered, for 2 hours.

For the turkey, position the oven rack to the lower third of the oven. Pat the turkey dry with paper towels. Place the turkey on a rack in a large roasting pan. Loosen the skin of the turkey. Rub 1/2 cup of the prepared maple herb butter under the turkey skin, over the breast meat. Rub remaining prepared butter over the outside of the turkey.

Truss the turkey. Arrange the onions, celery, carrot and reserved neck and giblets around the turkey in the pan. Sprinkle the remaining marjoram and thyme on the vegetables. Pour the chicken broth into the pan.

Bake at 375 degrees for 30 minutes. Reduce the heat to 350 degrees and tent the turkey with foil, covering completely. Roast for 2 hours and 25 minutes or until 180 degrees on a meat thermometer and the juices run clear when thickest part of the thigh is pierced with a skewer, basting occasionally. Transfer the turkey to a serving platter, tent with foil and let stand for 30 minutes before serving. *Yield: 12 servings.*

Baked Butternut Squash

2 medium (2¹/₂ pounds) butternut
    squash, peeled, seeded, quartered
6 cups chopped peeled Granny Smith
    apples
³/₄ cup dried currants
Nutmeg to taste

Salt to taste
Pepper to taste
³/₄ cup pure maple syrup
¹/₄ cup (¹/₂ stick) butter, cut into pieces
1¹/₂ tablespoons fresh lemon juice

Cook the squash in a large pot of boiling water for about 3 minutes or until almost tender; do not overcook. Drain well. Combine the squash, apples and currants in a 9×13-inch baking dish. Sprinkle with nutmeg, salt and pepper. Combine the maple syrup, butter and lemon juice in a small saucepan. Cook over low heat, whisking until the butter melts. Pour the syrup mixture over the squash mixture, stirring to coat evenly. Bake at 350 degrees for 1 hour or until the squash and apples are very tender; stir occasionally. Let cool for 5 minutes before serving. *Yield: 12 servings.*

Cranberry Salad

1 package fresh cranberries
1 apple, chopped
Zest of ¹/₂ orange
2 cups sugar
Juice of 2 oranges
³/₄ cup chopped pecans

1 (6-ounce) package lemon gelatin
1 (6-ounce) package cherry gelatin
3¹/₂ cups hot water
1 cup cold water
1 envelope unflavored gelatin
¹/₄ cup cold water

Combine the cranberries, apple and orange zest in a food processor container. Process until very finely chopped. Combine the cranberry mixture, sugar, orange juice and pecans in a large bowl; set aside.

Dissolve the lemon gelatin and cherry gelatin in 3¹/₂ cups hot water in a large bowl and add 1 cup cold water. Stir until the gelatin is dissolved. Combine the unflavored gelatin and ¹/₄ cup cold water in a small bowl . Add to the flavored gelatin mixture. Combine the cranberry mixture and gelatin mixture and pour into a large dish or gelatin mold. Chill, covered, until firm. *Yield: 16 servings.*

Pumpkin Chiffon Pie

1 envelope unflavored gelatin
1/2 cup sugar
1 teaspoon cinnamon
1/2 teaspoon salt
1/2 teaspoon nutmeg
1/2 teaspoon ginger
1/8 teaspoon cloves
2/3 cup evaporated milk

3 eggs, separated
1 1/4 cups canned pumpkin
1/4 cup sugar
2 baked (9-inch) pie shells
1 cup whipping cream, whipped
Nutmeg to taste

Combine the gelatin, 1/2 cup sugar, cinnamon, salt, 1/2 teaspoon nutmeg, ginger and cloves in a saucepan. Stir in the evaporated milk and egg yolks. Cook over medium-low heat for 10 minutes or until the gelatin dissolves and the mixture thickens, stirring constantly. Remove from the heat and stir in the pumpkin. Chill, covered, until cold. Beat the egg whites in a mixing bowl until soft peaks form. Add 1/4 cup sugar, gradually, and beat until stiff peaks form. Fold in the pumpkin mixture gently. Spoon into the pie shells. Chill until set. Spread the whipped cream over the top of the pies, sealing to the edge. Sprinkle with nutmeg to taste. *Yield: 16 servings.*

Wassail Punch

1 gallon apple cider
1 quart orange juice
1 cup lemon juice
1 quart pineapple juice
24 whole cloves

4 cinnamon sticks
1 cup sugar
1 package red hot cinnamon candies

Combine the apple cider, orange juice, lemon juice, pineapple juice, cloves, cinnamon sticks, sugar and candies in a large stockpot. Bring to a boil and simmer for 10 minutes, stirring constantly. Strain to remove the cloves and cinnamon sticks. Serve warm. For a festive punch bowl, float small oranges that have been studded with whole cloves in the punch.
Yield: 1 1/2 gallons (16 servings).

Football
Tailgating Party

Ham and Rolls

White Bean Chili

Barbecue Sandwiches

Green Bean Salad with Basil Vinaigrette

Raspberry Bars

Molasses Ginger Cookies

Ham and Rolls

2 packages Pepperidge Farm
  party rolls
16 ounces thinly sliced ham
8 ounces sliced Swiss cheese
1/2 cup (1 stick) butter, melted

1 1/2 tablespoons dry mustard
1 tablespoon onion flakes
1 tablespoon poppy seeds
1 1/2 teaspoons Worcestershire sauce

Split the party rolls in half; do not separate into individual rolls or remove from the trays. Layer the ham and cheese over the bottom half of the rolls. Place the top half of the rolls on top of the ham and cheese. Combine the melted butter, dry mustard, onion flakes, poppy seeds and Worcestershire sauce in a bowl and mix well. Pour the butter mixture evenly over the top of the rolls in each tray. Cover with aluminum foil. Chill for up to 8 hours. Bake at 350 degrees for 15 to 20 minutes. Serve immediately. *Yield: 20 servings.*

White Bean Chili

1 garlic clove, minced
1/2 cup chopped onion
1 tablespoon olive oil
4 boneless skinless chicken breasts
1 (10-ounce) can chicken broth
3 (15-ounce) cans Great Northern
    beans

1 (4-ounce) can chopped green chiles
1 tablespoon chopped fresh cilantro
1 1/2 tablespoons cumin
1/2 teaspoon salt
1/4 teaspoon freshly ground pepper

Sauté the garlic and onion in the olive oil in a Dutch oven until tender. Remove the garlic and onion from the pot and keep warm. Brown the chicken breasts on both sides in the olive oil in the pot. Add 1/2 can of the chicken broth. Simmer, covered, for 20 minutes. Remove the chicken and cut into bite-size pieces. Return the chicken to the pot. Add the remaining 1/2 can of the chicken broth and sautéed onion and garlic to the pot and mix well. Add the beans, green chiles, cilantro, cumin, salt and pepper and mix well.

Simmer, covered, for 20 to 30 minutes. Ladle into bowls to serve. Top with shredded Monterey Jack cheese, salsa and sour cream. Serve with tortilla chips. *Yield: 6 to 8 servings.*

Barbecue Sandwiches

1 (3-pound) boneless pork loin roast
1 cup water
1 (18-ounce) bottle barbecue sauce
1/4 cup packed brown sugar
2 tablespoons Worcestershire sauce

1 to 2 tablespoons hot red pepper sauce
1 teaspoon salt
1 teaspoon pepper
Sandwich buns
Coleslaw

Place the pork roast in a 4-quart slow cooker. Pour the water over the roast. Cook, covered, on High for 7 hours or until the roast is tender and shreds easily with a fork. Shred the roast into bite-size pieces with a fork. Add the barbecue sauce, brown sugar, Worcestershire sauce, hot sauce, salt and pepper and mix well. Reduce the heat to Low. Cook, covered, for 1 hour. Serve on the sandwich buns with coleslaw. *Yield: 20 servings.*

Green Bean Salad with Basil Vinaigrette

2 pounds fresh green beans, trimmed
3 shallots, minced
2 tablespoons balsamic or red wine
    vinegar
1/4 cup olive oil

2/3 cup chopped fresh basil
2/3 cup grated Romano cheese
Salt to taste
Pepper to taste

Cook the green beans in a large pot of boiling salted water to cover until tender-crisp. Rinse with cold water; drain. Combine the shallots and vinegar in a bowl. Whisk in the olive oil gradually. Stir in the basil. Pour over the green beans in a large bowl. Toss to coat well. Stir in the Romano cheese. Season with salt and pepper. Chill, covered, until serving time. Top with additional cheese if desired immediately before serving. *Yield: 6 servings.*

Raspberry Bars

1 cup flour
1 teaspoon baking powder
1/2 cup (1 stick) chilled butter,
  cut into pieces
2 eggs

1 tablespoon milk
1/2 cup raspberry jam
2/3 cup sugar
1/4 cup (1/2 stick) butter, melted
2 cups flaked coconut

Combine the flour and baking powder in a large bowl. Cut 1/2 cup butter into the flour mixture with a pastry blender until coarse crumbs form. Stir in the eggs 1 at a time. Add the milk and stir until a soft dough forms. Spread the dough evenly in a greased 8-inch square pan. Spread the jam evenly over the dough. Combine the sugar and 1/4 cup melted butter in a bowl and mix well. Stir in the coconut. Spread evenly over the jam layer. Bake at 350 degrees for 30 minutes or until light brown. Let cool and cut into bars to serve. Yield: 16 servings.

 Try substituting apricot, peach, or strawberry jam in place of the raspberry jam for different flavored treats.

Molasses Ginger Cookies

1 cup packed brown sugar
1/4 cup molasses
2/3 cup vegetable oil
1 egg, beaten
1 to 1 1/4 cups unbleached all-purpose
  flour
1 cup whole wheat flour

2 tablespoons soy flour
2 teaspoons baking soda
1 teaspoon cinnamon
1 teaspoon salt
1/2 teaspoon ginger
1/2 to 1 cup sugar

Combine the brown sugar, molasses, oil and egg in a large bowl and mix well. Combine the unbleached flour, wheat flour, soy flour, baking soda, cinnamon, salt and ginger in a large bowl. Add the flour mixture to the brown sugar mixture and mix well. Shape the dough into small balls or use a cookie scoop. Roll the balls in the sugar, coating well, and place on lightly greased cookie sheets. Bake at 350 degrees for 15 minutes or until light brown. Serve with a glass of cold milk or dress up a bowl of ice cream and fruit. Either way, they will go fast. Yield: 4 1/2 dozen.

International Spring Dinner

North African Orange Salad

Savory Green Beans with Coconut

African Green Pepper and Spinach

Shrimp Curry or Algerian Chicken

Lemon Hazelnut Squares

Ginger Tea

North African Orange Salad

6 blood oranges
2 tablespoons confectioners' sugar
1/2 teaspoon cinnamon
1/4 cup olive oil
3 tablespoons fresh lemon juice

1/2 teaspoon cumin
Pinch of salt
3 bunches watercress, trimmed
18 Morrocan or cured black olives,
   pitted, sliced

Grate the zest of 1 orange; set aside. Remove the peel and white pith of each orange and slice into segments; remove all the seeds. Combine the confectioners' sugar and cinnamon in a shaker with a wire mesh top; set aside. Combine the olive oil, lemon juice, cumin, salt and orange zest in a large bowl. Add the watercress and olives and toss to coat well. Divide among 6 salad plates. Top each plate with the orange segments. Sprinkle with the sugar-cinnamon mixture. Serve immediately. *Yield: 6 servings.*

Savory Green Beans with Coconut

1/2 cup flaked coconut
1/2 cup water
1 medium onion, sliced
1 teaspoon coriander
1/2 teaspoon turmeric

1/2 teaspoon ginger
1/4 cup clarified unsalted butter
1 1/2 pounds fresh green beans,
 trimmed and French-cut
1 1/2 teaspoons salt

Combine the coconut and water in a blender container and process until the coconut is very finely chopped; set aside. Sauté the onion, coriander, turmeric and ginger in the clarified butter in a skillet over medium heat until the onion is well coated. Stir in the coconut, beans and salt. Cook, covered, over medium heat for 10 to 25 minutes or until beans are tender-crisp. Yield: 4 or 5 servings.

 To clarify butter, melt at least 1 cup unsalted butter in a skillet over low heat. Let simmer for 20 to 25 minutes. The white milk solids will collect at the bottom. Skim off any foam from the top. Remove from the heat and pour the clear, golden liquid through a fine sieve into a glass jar, discarding the white milk solids left in the pan or sieve. Cool completely. The clarified butter will keep for up to 3 months tightly sealed in the refrigerator.

African Green Pepper and Spinach

1 medium green bell pepper, chopped
1 medium onion, chopped
1 tablespoon vegetable oil
1 medium tomato, chopped

1 pound fresh spinach, trimmed
3/4 teaspoon salt
1/8 teaspoon pepper
1/4 cup creamy peanut butter

Sauté the bell pepper and onion in the oil in a 3-quart saucepan until tender. Add the tomato and spinach. Simmer, covered, for 5 minutes or until tender. Stir in the salt, pepper and peanut butter. Cook until heated through. Yield: 4 servings.

Shrimp Curry

2 pounds fresh peeled shrimp
Vegetable oil
3 small onions, chopped
5 garlic cloves, minced
2 stalks lemon grass, chopped
1/2 teaspoon turmeric
1/2 teaspoon cumin
1/2 teaspoon sugar

1/4 teaspoon ginger
1/8 teaspoon black pepper
1/2 teaspoon cinnamon
1 teaspoon salt
Cayenne pepper to taste
2 bay leaves
5 tomatoes, finely chopped
2 to 3 cups light coconut milk

Sauté the shrimp in a small amount of oil in a skillet until pink; remove the shrimp and set aside. Sauté the onions, garlic and lemon grass in the skillet until tender. Add the turmeric, cumin, sugar, ginger, black pepper, cinnamon, salt, cayenne pepper and bay leaves and cook for 5 to 10 minutes. Stir in the tomatoes and cook for 10 minutes. Add the coconut milk and cook for 10 minutes or until thickened. Add the shrimp and cook for 10 minutes. Remove the bay leaves. Serve immediately over hot cooked white rice. *Yield: 6 servings.*

Algerian Chicken

2 medium onions, thinly sliced,
  separated into rings
1 medium green bell pepper, thinly
  sliced
3/4 cup sliced fresh mushrooms
1 tablespoon water
2 teaspoons oregano
2 teaspoons crushed red pepper

1 teaspoon garlic salt
1/2 teaspoon hot red pepper sauce
1 (14-ounce) can tomatoes
2/3 cup peanut butter
2 teaspoons instant chicken bouillon
  granules
8 boneless skinless chicken breasts

Combine the onions, bell pepper, mushrooms, water, oregano, red pepper, garlic salt and hot red pepper sauce in a large skillet. Cook over medium heat until the vegetables are tender-crisp, stirring frequently. Combine the tomatoes, peanut butter and bouillon in a blender container. Process until smooth. Place the chicken in a 9×13-inch baking dish. Top with the prepared vegetable mixture. Pour the blended tomato mixture over the top. Bake, covered, at 350 degrees for 1 hour or until chicken tests done. Serve the chicken over hot cooked rice. Spoon the sauce over the top. *Yield: 8 servings.*

Lemon Hazelnut Squares

1 cup flour
1/4 cup sugar
1/4 teaspoon salt
6 tablespoons chilled unsalted butter,
    cut into pieces
1/4 cup chopped toasted hazelnuts

3/4 cup sugar
2 eggs
3 tablespoons fresh lemon juice
1 tablespoon grated lemon zest
1/2 teaspoon baking powder
Confectioners' sugar

Combine the flour, 1/4 cup sugar and salt in a food processor container. Add the butter and hazelnuts and process until fine crumbs form. Press into the bottom of a greased 8-inch baking pan. Bake at 350 degrees for 18 minutes or until the edges begin to brown. Set aside.

Combine 3/4 cup sugar, eggs, lemon juice, lemon zest and baking powder in a food processor container. Process until well blended. Pour evenly over the prepared crust. Bake at 350 degrees for 20 minutes or until the edges begin to brown and the filling is set. Let cool before cutting into squares. Sprinkle confectioners' sugar over the squares before serving. Yield: 16 servings.

Ginger Tea

3 tablespoons instant unsweetened tea
1 1/2 cups sugar
2 cups orange juice
1 (6-ounce) can frozen limeade or
    lemonade concentrate, thawed

6 cups water
40 ounces ginger ale

Combine the instant tea, sugar, orange juice, limeade concentrate, water and ginger ale in a large container and mix well until the instant tea and sugar are dissolved. You may add more water if desired. Chill until serving time. Serve cold. Yield: 1 to 1 1/2 gallons (20 servings).

Appetizers

sarah rally s. schuyler

Sarah Tallu S. Schuyler

Sarah Tallu S. Schuyler is a native of Pittsburgh, Pennsylvania, and a graduate of Penn State University. She continued her art studies at Carnegie Mellon University in Pittsburgh, and The Art Students League in New York City. Sarah has taught at Carnegie Mellon, Chautauqua Institute in New York, Ivy School of Art in Pittsburgh, and many classes in the Nashville, Tennessee, area. She lives in Nashville with her husband and three children.

Shown on overleaf: *Evening Pear*

Black Bean Salsa

2 (15-ounce) cans black beans, rinsed, drained
1 (11-ounce) can Shoe Peg corn, drained
3 firm tomatoes, peeled, seeded, chopped
1 cup finely chopped fresh cilantro
1/4 cup fresh lime juice
8 drops Tabasco sauce
2 tablespoons balsamic vinegar
Salt to taste
Pepper to taste
3 avocados, pitted, chopped

Combine the beans, corn, tomatoes and cilantro in a large bowl and mix well. Stir in the lime juice, Tabasco sauce and balsamic vinegar. Add the salt and pepper and mix well. Chill, covered, until serving time. Add the avocados immediately before serving. Toss to combine. Serve with tortilla chips. *Yield: 8 servings.*

 Try combining chopped, cooked chicken, shredded cheese, and Black Bean Salsa and spooning onto a flour tortilla. Roll up and place on a baking sheet. Bake at 375 degrees for 15 to 20 minutes or until golden around the edges. Serve as a main dish or cut into smaller pieces for easy appetizers.

Roasted Red Bell Pepper and Artichoke Dip

2 teaspoons butter or margarine
1/3 cup chopped green onions
1 (14-ounce) can artichoke hearts, drained, chopped
1 cup mayonnaise
1 cup grated Parmesan cheese
1 (7-ounce) jar roasted red bell peppers, chopped
1/8 teaspoon pepper
2 tablespoons grated Parmesan cheese
1 tablespoon chopped fresh parsley

Heat the butter in a skillet. Sauté the green onions in the hot butter in the skillet until tender. Remove from the heat. Stir in the artichoke hearts, mayonnaise, 1 cup Parmesan cheese, roasted bell peppers and pepper. Spoon into a 9-inch round baking dish, spreading evenly. Sprinkle with 2 tablespoons Parmesan cheese and parsley.

Bake at 350 degrees for 20 minutes or until bubbly. Serve hot with assorted crackers. You may substitute 1 roasted and chopped red bell pepper for the jar of roasted red bell peppers. This may be assembled 24 hours in advance and chilled. Bake immediately before serving time. Yield: 12 servings.

 Prepare cold dips at least 1 hour ahead or even a day in advance to allow the flavors to blend. Hot dips may be assembled ahead, covered, and kept refrigerated until ready to bake.

Cold Artichoke Dip

2 (14-ounce) cans artichoke hearts, drained, chopped
2/3 cup mayonnaise
1 tablespoon chopped onion
3 to 4 slices bacon, crisp-cooked, crumbled
Juice of 1/2 lemon
Salt to taste
Black pepper to taste
Red pepper to taste

Combine the artichoke hearts, mayonnaise, onion, bacon, lemon juice, salt, black pepper and red pepper in a bowl and mix well. Chill, covered, until serving time. Serve cold with corn chips. You may double the bacon if desired. Yield: 6 to 8 servings.

Vidalia Onion Dip

4 to 5 large Vidalia onions, finely chopped
24 ounces cream cheese, softened
1/2 cup mayonnaise
1/4 cup sour cream
2 cups grated Parmesan cheese

Combine the onions, cream cheese, mayonnaise, sour cream and Parmesan cheese in a large bowl and mix well. Spoon into a baking dish. Bake at 375 degrees for 45 minutes. Serve hot with corn chips. This may be prepared 1 day in advance and chilled. Bake immediately before serving time. You may also prepare using frozen chopped onions. Yield: 15 servings.

Swiss Bacon Dip

8 ounces cream cheese, softened
1 cup shredded Swiss cheese
1/2 cup mayonnaise
2 tablespoons chopped green onions
1/4 teaspoon paprika
8 slices bacon, crisp-cooked, crumbled
1/2 cup crushed butter crackers

Combine the cream cheese, Swiss cheese, mayonnaise, green onions and paprika in a bowl and mix well. Spoon into a small baking dish. Mix the bacon and butter cracker crumbs in a small bowl. Sprinkle evenly over the top. Bake at 350 degrees for 20 minutes. Serve hot with assorted crackers. *Yield: 6 servings.*

Basil Tomato Tapenade

1/2 cup chopped Kalamata olives
1/2 cup chopped sun-dried tomatoes
1/4 cup extra-virgin olive oil
1/4 cup fresh basil, sliced into thin strips
1 tablespoon capers

Combine the olives, tomatoes, olive oil, basil and capers in a small glass bowl; mix well. Chill, covered, until serving time. Serve on top of toasted bread rounds or spoon on top of cream cheese or goat cheese for a spread.

You may also toss with hot cooked pasta. This tapenade will keep for up to 10 days, covered, in the refrigerator. *Yield: 6 servings.*

Feta and Sun-Dried Tomato Torta

1/2 pound (2 sticks) unsalted butter, cut into pieces
3 cups crumbled feta cheese
8 ounces cream cheese, softened
2 garlic cloves, minced
1 shallot, minced
Freshly ground white pepper to taste
Hot red pepper sauce to taste
1/2 cup toasted pine nuts
8 ounces sun-dried tomatoes soaked in olive oil, chopped
1 cup prepared pesto

Combine the butter, feta cheese, cream cheese, garlic, shallot, white pepper and hot pepper sauce in a food processor container. Process until smooth. Grease a 4- to 5-cup straight-sided mold or bowl. Line with plastic wrap, leaving enough hanging over the sides to fold over.

Layer the pine nuts, sun-dried tomatoes, pesto and prepared butter mixture in the prepared mold. Fold the plastic wrap over the top and press gently to compact the layers. Chill until firm, 1 hour or more. Invert onto a serving platter and remove the plastic wrap. Serve with bagel chips, toasted pita triangles or toasted bread rounds. *Yield: 20 servings.*

Layered Cheese Loaf

1 (10-ounce) package frozen chopped spinach, thawed, drained
16 ounces sharp Cheddar cheese, shredded
1/2 cup toasted chopped pecans
1/2 cup mayonnaise
8 ounces cream cheese, softened
Salt to taste
Pepper to taste
8 ounces cream cheese, softened
1/4 cup chutney
1/4 teaspoon nutmeg

Press the spinach between paper towels to remove all the excess moisture; set aside. Combine the shredded Cheddar cheese, pecans and mayonnaise in a small bowl and mix well. Spread half of the mixture into a 5×9-inch loaf pan lined with plastic wrap. Combine the spinach, 8 ounces cream cheese, salt and pepper in a small bowl and mix well.

Spread evenly over the Cheddar cheese layer. Combine 8 ounces cream cheese, chutney and nutmeg in a small bowl and mix well. Spread evenly over the spinach layer. Top with the remaining Cheddar cheese mixture and spread evenly. Cover and freeze for up to 1 month. Thaw before serving. Garnish as desired and serve with assorted crackers. *Yield: 25 servings.*

Mushroom Pâté

1 pound sliced mushrooms
2 tablespoons butter or margarine
2 tablespoons red wine
8 ounces cream cheese, softened
1 teaspoon seasoned pepper
1/2 teaspoon garlic salt

Sauté the sliced mushrooms in the butter and wine in a skillet over medium-high heat under tender. Drain the mushrooms and let cool. Combine the mushrooms, cream cheese, seasoned pepper and garlic salt in a blender or food processor container. Process until smooth.

Line a 3×71/2-inch loaf pan with plastic wrap. Spoon the mushroom mixture into the prepared pan. Chill, covered, until serving time. Invert onto a serving plate and remove the plastic wrap. Garnish with fresh rosemary if desired. Serve with toasted French bread slices. Yield: 8 to 10 servings.

Marinated Asparagus

1/2 cup sugar
1/2 cup water
2/3 cup vinegar
1 tablespoon celery seeds
3 cinnamon sticks
1 teaspoon whole cloves
1/2 teaspoon salt
2 bunches steamed fresh asparagus

Combine the sugar, water, vinegar, celery seeds, cinnamon sticks, cloves and salt in a small saucepan. Bring to a boil. Pour over the asparagus in a shallow dish. Chill, covered, for 24 to 48 hours. Drain the asparagus before serving. Serve cold. Yield: 8 to 10 servings.

Chicken and Brie Quesadillas

2 cups chopped plum tomatoes
1 small onion, chopped
3 tablespoons fresh lime juice
2 teaspoons minced chipotle chiles
5 green onions, minced
$1/2$ teaspoon salt
$1/2$ cup chopped fresh cilantro
1 cup finely chopped cooked chicken
1 ($4^1/2$-ounce) can chopped green chiles
8 flour tortillas
8 ounces Brie cheese, trimmed, chopped

Combine the tomatoes, onion, lime juice, chipotle chiles, $1/4$ cup green onions, salt and $1/4$ cup cilantro in a small bowl and chill the salsa, covered, for 1 hour. Combine the remaining green onions, remaining cilantro, chicken and green chiles in a bowl and mix well.

Place 4 flour tortillas on a large baking sheet. Arrange the Brie cheese and chicken mixture on each tortilla. Cover with the remaining 4 tortillas and press gently. Bake at 350 degrees for 10 minutes. Cut into triangles and serve with the prepared salsa. *Yield: 8 servings*.

Spinach Roll

1 bunch green onions, chopped
  (including green tops)
1/4 cup (1/2 stick) butter
4 (10-ounce) packages frozen chopped
  spinach, cooked, drained
1/4 cup chopped fresh parsley
1 1/2 to 2 pounds Monterey Jack cheese,
  shredded
1/3 cup grated Parmesan cheese

1 1/2 tablespoons dillseeds
6 eggs, beaten
1/4 teaspoon salt
1/4 teaspoon pepper
1 (16-ounce) package frozen phyllo
  dough, thawed according to
  package directions
1 1/2 cups (3 sticks) butter, melted

Sauté the green onions in 1/4 cup butter in a skillet until tender. Combine the green onions, spinach, parsley, Monterey Jack cheese, Parmesan cheese, dillseeds, eggs, salt and pepper in a bowl and mix well. Divide the mixture into 4 equal portions; set aside. Lay a slightly damp towel over the thawed phyllo dough if it becomes too dry. Remove 1 sheet of dough at a time. Brush 1 side with the melted butter and place on a work surface.

Lay a second sheet of dough on top of the first one and carefully brush with the melted butter. Repeat until 5 sheets of dough are prepared and on top of each other. Place 1 portion of the prepared spinach mixture along the long edge of the dough. Roll up the dough, tucking in the edge as you roll. Repeat the process with the remaining dough and spinach mixture.

Place each prepared roll on a baking sheet. Brush the rolls with melted butter. Bake at 350 degrees for 45 minutes or until golden brown. Cut into slices to serve. The pastry will be very flaky. *Yield: 20 to 24 servings*.

Favorite Party Pork Tenderloins

1 cup light soy sauce
2 tablespoons brown sugar
1¹/₂ tablespoons bourbon
2 (³/₄-pound) pork tenderloins, trimmed

Combine the soy sauce, brown sugar and bourbon in a small bowl and mix well. Place the pork tenderloins in a large sealable plastic bag and pour the marinade in the bag. Marinate in the refrigerator for 1 hour, turning the bag every 15 minutes. Remove the tenderloins to a nonaluminum broiler pan. Pour the marinade over the tenderloins.

Bake at 300 degrees for 1 hour or until 170 degrees on a meat thermometer, spooning juices over the tenderloins every 15 minutes. Let cool slightly before slicing; reserve the marinade. Place the slices in a chafing dish and pour the marinade over the slices; keep warm. Serve with yeast rolls and let guests spoon the sauce over the slices on the rolls. *Yield: 12 to 15 servings.*

Thinly slice the Favorite Party Pork Tenderloins and serve 2 to 3 slices over warm cranberry chutney. Top with crumbled bleu cheese and toasted walnuts. Garnish with fresh chopped chives and serve as an elegant entrée.

Crab Swiss Bites

1 (7¹/2-ounce) can crab meat, drained, flaked
1 (5-ounce) can water chestnuts, drained, finely chopped
2 tablespoons finely chopped green onions
1 cup shredded Swiss cheese
¹/2 cup mayonnaise
1 teaspoon lemon juice
¹/2 teaspoon curry powder
1 (10-count) can refrigerator biscuits

Combine the crab meat, water chestnuts, green onions, Swiss cheese, mayonnaise, lemon juice and curry powder in a bowl and mix well. Separate each biscuit into 3 pieces and place on a baking sheet; flatten slightly. Spoon a small amount of the crab mixture onto each biscuit round. Bake at 400 degrees for 10 to 12 minutes or until golden brown. Serve hot.
Yield: 30 servings.

Crab Cakes

¹/4 cup reduced-fat mayonnaise
¹/4 cup finely chopped celery
¹/4 cup finely chopped green onions
¹/4 cup finely chopped fresh parsley
2 tablespoons fresh lemon or lime juice
1 teaspoon (or more) hot red pepper sauce
1 teaspoon (or more) Dijon mustard
1 pound lump crab meat or imitation crab meat, flaked
¹/4 cup bread crumbs
Salt to taste
Pepper to taste
³/4 cup bread crumbs
2 teaspoons vegetable oil

Combine the mayonnaise, celery, green onions, parsley, lemon juice, hot red pepper sauce, mustard, crab meat and ¹/4 cup bread crumbs in a large bowl and mix well. Season with the salt and pepper. Shape the mixture into 12 patties; the mixture will be soft. Coat each patty with the remaining ³/4 cup bread crumbs. Heat the oil in a large skillet.

Cook the crab cakes in the hot oil for 2 to 3 minutes on each side or until golden brown. Serve with salsa. To serve the crab cakes as an entrée, shape the mixture into 8 larger patties. Each serving is 2 patties. Yield: 12 servings.

Barbecue Basil Shrimp

8 fresh deveined peeled jumbo shrimp
8 fresh basil leaves
4 strips smoked bacon, cut in half
1 cup thick high-quality barbecue sauce
1 tablespoon freshly ground horseradish
1 tablespoon honey
1 tablespoon freshly ground pepper

Wrap each shrimp carefully with 1 basil leaf and 1/2 piece of bacon. Secure with a wooden pick. Place the prepared shrimp on a baking sheet. Bake at 375 degrees for 8 to 10 minutes, turning once. Turn the oven to broil and brown the shrimp for 3 to 4 minutes.

Remove from the oven and keep warm. Combine the barbecue sauce, horseradish, honey and pepper in a blender container and process for 1 minute. Pour the sauce into a bowl. Add the shrimp and toss lightly to coat with the sauce. Serve with lemon wedges and fresh parsley.
Yield: 8 servings.

Thai Shrimp

3 tablespoons sunflower oil
2 tablespoons Thai fish sauce
2 stalks lemon grass, finely chopped
1 red chile, finely chopped
2 tablespoons chopped fresh cilantro
1 tablespoon grated fresh gingerroot
20 fresh deveined peeled shrimp
    with tails

1 teaspoon sugar
1 tablespoon soy sauce
1 red chile, finely chopped
1 tablespoon Thai fish sauce
Juice of 1 large lime
2 green onions, chopped
1 tablespoon chopped fresh cilantro

Combine the sunflower oil, 2 tablespoons fish sauce, lemon grass, 1 red chile, 2 tablespoons cilantro and gingerroot in a bowl and mix well. Add the shrimp and toss to coat well. Marinate, covered, in the refrigerator for 1 hour. Remove the shrimp and thread onto wooden skewers that have been soaked in cold water for 1 hour. Pour the marinade into a saucepan. Add the sugar, soy sauce, 1 red chile, 1 tablespoon fish sauce and lime juice.

Bring to a boil and boil for 1 minute. Remove the dipping sauce from the heat and let cool. Stir in the green onions and 1 tablespoon cilantro. Grill the shrimp on a lightly greased grill rack over hot coals for 2 to 3 minutes on each side until shrimp are pink. Do not overcook. Serve with the prepared dipping sauce. *Yield: 10 servings.*

Cheddar Cheese Toast

¹/2 cup (1 stick) butter, softened
2 cups shredded sharp Cheddar cheese
2 eggs
1 teaspoon garlic salt
1 teaspoon onion salt
Sourdough or French bread loaves, sliced

Beat the butter in a mixing bowl until creamy. Add the cheese, eggs, garlic salt and onion salt and beat until well mixed. Spread on bread slices. Place the bread slices on a baking sheet. Bake at 350 degrees for 15 minutes. Serve hot. These can be prepared ahead and frozen. Thaw before baking. *Yield: Variable.*

Cheese Wafers

¹/2 cup (1 stick) butter, softened
2 cups shredded sharp Cheddar cheese
1 cup finely chopped pecans
1¹/2 cups flour
Cayenne pepper to taste

Combine the butter and cheese in a large bowl and mix well. Add the pecans, flour and cayenne pepper and mix well. Shape into 3 logs. Wrap in waxed paper and chill for 8 hours. Slice into thin wafers and place on a baking sheet. Bake at 425 degrees for 10 minutes or until light brown. Store in an airtight container. *Yield: 2 dozen.*

Pita Chips

1 (12-ounce) package pita rounds
1/3 to 1/2 cup fresh chopped chives
2 garlic cloves, minced
1 cup olive oil
1/3 cup grated Parmesan cheese
Dash of Tabasco sauce

Separate the pita bread rounds. Combine the chives, garlic, olive oil, Parmesan cheese and Tabasco sauce in a food processor container. Process until well blended and of sauce-like consistency. Brush 1 tablespoon of the olive oil mixture over each round with a pastry brush. Cut each round into 8 wedges using a pizza cutter. Place the wedges on a baking sheet.

Bake at 400 degrees for 7 to 10 minutes or until light brown. Do not underbake; make sure the pita chips are crisp. Remove to wire racks to cool. Store in an airtight container for up to 1 week. Serve with spreads, soft cheese or alone as a snack. Yield: 20 servings.

Soft Pretzels

1 1/4 cups milk
3 cups flour
1/4 cup sugar
1 envelope dry yeast
1 teaspoon baking powder

1 teaspoon garlic salt
1/2 cup (1 stick) unsalted butter, melted
1 cup flour
2 quarts (8 cups) water
2 tablespoons baking soda

Heat the milk in a saucepan over low heat until 120 to 130 degrees on a thermometer. Combine 3 cups flour, sugar, yeast, baking powder and garlic salt in a large mixing bowl. Add the heated milk and melted butter. Beat for 2 minutes. Add 1 cup flour 1/4 cup at a time, beating until the dough pulls away from the side of the bowl. Turn the dough out onto a lightly floured surface. Flatten slightly. Knead for 10 minutes or until the dough is smooth and elastic, adding more flour if necessary to prevent sticking. Shape into a ball and place in a large lightly greased bowl, turning to coat the surface. Let rise, covered, in a warm place for 30 minutes.

Divide the dough into 15 to 18 equal pieces. Roll each piece into a 22-inch long rope on a greased surface. Form the rope into a "U" shape and cross the surface about 2 inches from each end. Cross the dough a second time. Fold the ends up to the rounded part of the "U"; pressing the ends to seal. Turn the pretzel over so that the ends are underside and reshape if necessary. Let stand, covered, for 20 minutes. Pour the water into a large stockpot. Add the baking soda.

Bring the water to a boil over high heat. Drop 3 pretzels at a time carefully into the boiling water. Boil for 10 seconds. Remove with a slotted spoon. Place on a well-greased baking sheet. Sprinkle the pretzels with coarse salt or sesame seeds. Bake at 400 degrees for 15 minutes or until golden brown. Remove to a wire rack to cool. *Yield: Variable.*

Brunch & Beverages

STREATER SPENCER

Streater Odom Spencer

Streater Odom Spencer holds a marketing degree from the University of Mississippi, and studied art in Atlanta with the late Ben Shute, co-founder of the Atlanta College of Art. After moving to Nashville, Tennessee, in 1987, she began showing and selling her works. Streater works in oil, and shows in various galleries throughout the Southeast.

Shown on overleaf: *Simple Pleasures*

Serbian Eggs

1/2 cup (1 stick) margarine
6 eggs, beaten
1 cup baking mix
2 tablespoons flour

1 cup milk
2 cups cottage cheese
2 cups shredded Colby cheese
2 cups shredded Monterey Jack cheese

Melt the margarine in a 9×13-inch baking dish in a 375-degree oven.
Combine the eggs, baking mix, flour and milk in a large bowl and mix well.
Add the cottage cheese, Colby cheese and Monterey Jack cheese and mix
well. Pour in the melted margarine; mix well. Pour the egg mixture into the
prepared dish. Bake at 375 degrees for 40 minutes. Serve with salsa and
sour cream. *Yield: 12 servings.*

Ham and Sunflower Frittata

6 eggs, lightly beaten
3/4 cup plain yogurt or reduced-fat
  sour cream
Salt to taste
Freshly ground pepper to taste
1 cup finely chopped ham
2 green onions, chopped, including
  green tops

2 tablespoons minced fresh flat-leaf
  parsley
1/2 cup shredded Jarlsberg or Gruyère
  cheese
4 tablespoons sunflower seed kernels

Combine the eggs, yogurt, salt, pepper, ham, green onions, parsley,
cheese and 2 tablespoons of the sunflower seed kernels in a bowl; mix well.
Pour into a greased 9-inch square baking dish. Sprinkle with the remaining
2 tablespoons sunflower seed kernels. Bake at 350 degrees for 20 to 25
minutes or until set. Cut into squares to serve. Serve hot. *Yield: 8 servings.*

Breakfast Pizza

1 pound mild bulk pork sausage
2 (8-count) cans refrigerator crescent rolls
2 cups frozen hash brown potatoes, thawed
1 1/2 cups shredded Cheddar cheese
5 eggs
1/4 cup milk
1/2 teaspoon salt
1/8 teaspoon pepper
2 tablespoons grated Parmesan cheese

Brown the sausage in a large skillet, stirring until crumbly; drain. Unroll the crescent rolls onto a large pizza pan, pressing up the lip of the dough to form a crust; seal the perforations. Spoon the sausage onto the crust. Sprinkle with the hash brown potatoes. Top with the Cheddar cheese. Whisk the eggs, milk, salt and pepper in a bowl. Pour evenly over the top of the pizza. Sprinkle with the Parmesan cheese.

Bake at 375 degrees for 25 to 30 minutes. Cut into slices to serve. The pizza may be assembled the night before. Prepare the egg mixture in the morning, pour over the pizza and bake. *Yield: 8 servings.*

Classic Colorado Quiche

1 (1-crust) pie pastry
1 cup sliced fresh mushrooms
1 tablespoon butter
1 cup shredded Cheddar cheese
1 (10-ounce) package frozen chopped
    spinach, thawed, drained
3 eggs, beaten
1 1/2 cups heavy cream

2 teaspoons Worcestershire sauce
1/2 teaspoon sugar
1/2 teaspoon onion salt
1/4 teaspoon minced garlic
1/8 teaspoon freshly ground pepper
3 slices bacon, crisp-cooked, crumbled
1/3 cup freshly grated Parmesan cheese
3 slices bacon, crisp-cooked, crumbled

Fit the pie pastry into a deep-dish 10-inch pie pan. Press over the bottom and up the side. Trim and flute the edges and prick evenly with a fork. Line the pastry with foil. Place pie weights or dried beans in the pastry shell. Bake at 350 degrees for 5 minutes. Remove the weights and foil and let cool.

Sauté the mushrooms in the butter in a small skillet until tender; set aside. Sprinkle the Cheddar cheese evenly over the prepared pie shell. Combine the spinach, eggs, cream, Worcestershire sauce, sugar, onion salt, garlic and pepper in a large bowl and mix well. Stir in the prepared mushrooms and 3 slices of crumbled bacon. Pour into the prepared pie shell. Distribute the mushrooms and spinach evenly with a fork. Sprinkle with the Parmesan cheese.

Bake at 350 degrees for 20 minutes. Sprinkle with the remaining 3 slices of crumbled bacon. Bake at 350 degrees for 25 to 40 minutes or until a knife inserted in the center comes out clean. If quiche begins to brown too quickly, tent with foil. Let stand for 5 to 10 minutes before serving.
Yield: 6 to 8 servings.

Feta Quiche Florentine

3 eggs, beaten
1 (10-ounce) package frozen chopped spinach,
thawed, drained
3/4 cup milk
1/4 cup chopped green onions
8 ounces crumbled feta cheese
1/8 teaspoon pepper
1 unbaked (9-inch) pie shell
1 tomato, sliced

Combine the eggs, spinach, milk, onions, cheese and pepper in a bowl and mix well. Pour into the pie shell and top with the tomato slices. Bake at 350 degrees for 55 minutes. Let stand for 5 to 10 minutes before serving. Yield: 6 to 8 servings.

 The next time you make an omelet, try filling it with guacamole, shredded cheese, and chopped tomato—an easy and delicious breakfast.

Basil Soufflé

1 tablespoon butter
1 tablespoon freshly grated Parmesan cheese
1/4 cup (1/2 stick) butter
1/4 cup flour
1 teaspoon salt
1 1/4 cups milk
6 egg yolks
1 garlic clove
1/4 cup freshly grated Parmesan cheese
1/4 cup chopped walnuts
1 cup fresh basil leaves
2 tablespoons olive oil
6 egg whites

Grease a soufflé dish with 1 tablespoon butter. Sprinkle evenly with 1 tablespoon Parmesan cheese; set aside. Melt 1/4 cup butter in a saucepan over medium heat. Add the flour and salt, stirring constantly. Cook until roux thickens and smells toasted. Whisk in the milk quickly. Cook over medium heat until thickened. Remove from the heat and whisk in the egg yolks; set aside.

Mince the garlic in a food processor. Add 1/4 cup Parmesan cheese and process until finely grated. Add the walnuts and basil and process until finely chopped. Add the olive oil in a slow stream, processing until well blended. Add to the prepared white sauce and mix well.

Beat the egg whites in a mixing bowl until stiff. Fold into the white sauce mixture. Spoon into the prepared soufflé dish. Bake at 350 degrees for 25 to 30 minutes. This is a beautiful brunch dish served with coffee cake and fresh fruit. Yield: 6 to 8 servings.

Cheese Soufflé

3½ tablespoons butter
¼ cup flour
1½ cups milk
6 egg yolks
1 cup shredded Cheddar cheese
1 teaspoon dry mustard
Dash of cayenne pepper
2 to 3 drops of hot red pepper sauce
¼ cup grated Parmesan cheese
8 egg whites
Pinch of salt
⅛ teaspoon cream of tartar

Melt the butter in a saucepan over medium heat. Add the flour and stir until slightly thickened. Stir in the milk. Remove from the heat. Whisk in the egg yolks 1 at a time. Add the Cheddar cheese, dry mustard, cayenne pepper, hot sauce and Parmesan cheese and mix well; set aside. Beat the egg whites in a large mixing bowl with the salt and cream of tartar until stiff. Fold the cheese mixture into the egg whites. Spoon into a greased and floured soufflé dish.

Place in a 400-degree oven and immediately reduce the heat to 375 degrees. Bake for 30 minutes. You may also prepare in two smaller soufflé dishes or individual soufflé dishes. *Yield: 6 to 8 servings*.

Nana's Cheese Grits

6 cups water
1 1/2 cups grits
1/2 cup (1 stick) margarine, softened
3 eggs, beaten
3 cups shredded sharp Cheddar cheese
3 teaspoons seasoned salt

Boil the water in a saucepan and cook the grits according to the package directions. Remove from the heat and stir in the margarine, eggs, cheese and seasoned salt. Spoon into a greased 9×12-inch baking dish. Bake at 350 degrees for 30 to 40 minutes. *Yield: 12 servings.*

 Grits aren't just for breakfast anymore! Serve these Cheese Grits as a delicious side dish to chicken or seafood.

Featherlight Yogurt Pancakes

2 cups flour
2 teaspoons baking powder
1 teaspoon baking soda
1 tablespoon sugar
1 teaspoon salt
1 cup plain yogurt
1 to 1 1/4 cups milk
2 eggs, lightly beaten
1/4 cup (1/2 stick) butter, melted

Sift together the flour, baking powder, baking soda, sugar and salt in a large bowl. Combine the yogurt, milk and eggs in a large bowl and mix well. Stir in the melted butter.

Pour into the flour mixture and stir just until moistened. Pour 1/4 cup batter at a time onto a hot greased griddle. Cook until light brown on both sides, turning once. Serve hot with desired toppings. Yield: 16 servings.

 Have leftover pancakes from breakfast? Spread them with peanut butter and jelly and roll up for lunch.

German Pancakes

3 cups sifted flour
1/4 cup sugar
1/8 teaspoon salt
2 cups milk
3 eggs, beaten
Applesauce
Maple syrup

Combine the flour, sugar and salt in a large bowl. Make a well in the center of the flour mixture. Combine the milk and beaten eggs in a bowl and mix well. Fold the milk and egg mixture slowly into the well in the flour mixture. Stir until the mixture is very smooth. Pour 1/2 cup batter at a time onto a hot greased skillet. Roll to cover the pan with a thin layer of the batter. Cook until light brown on both sides, turning once.

The pancakes will be thin, similar to crepes. Store in a warm oven to keep soft. To serve, fill the thin pancakes with warm applesauce and roll up to enclose. Drizzle with warm syrup. Strawberry preserves and sour cream also make a delicious filling. *Yield: 24 servings.*

Honey Puffed Pancake

Pancake
1 cup milk
6 eggs
3 tablespoons honey
3 ounces cream cheese, softened
1 cup flour
$1/2$ teaspoon salt
$1/2$ teaspoon baking powder
3 tablespoons butter

Honey Butter Spread
$1/2$ cup (1 stick) butter, softened
$1/2$ cup honey
$1/2$ cup confectioners' sugar
Cinnamon to taste

For *the pancake*, combine the milk, eggs, honey, cream cheese, flour, salt and baking powder in a blender container. Process for 1 minute or until smooth. Grease a 10-inch ovenproof skillet with 1 tablespoon of the butter. Add the remaining 2 tablespoons butter to the skillet. Heat the skillet in a 400-degree oven until the butter sizzles. Pour the batter into the prepared skillet.

Bake at 400 degrees for 20 minutes or until the pancake is puffed and light brown. Pancake will flatten slightly as it cools.

For *the spread*, combine the butter, honey, confectioners' sugar and cinnamon in a bowl and mix until well blended. Cut the pancake into slices and serve with the Honey Butter Spread. *Yield: 6 servings.*

Saturday Morning Pancakes

3 eggs, lightly beaten
2 cups milk
2 cups baking mix
2 tablespoons oat bran
2 tablespoons wheat bran flakes

Whisk the eggs and milk together in a large bowl. Add the baking mix, oat bran and wheat bran flakes and whisk until smooth. The batter will thicken while standing. You may add more milk 1 tablespoon at a time if needed to thin the batter.

Pour batter 1/4 cup at a time onto a hot greased griddle. Cook until light brown on each side, turning once. Serve hot with maple syrup, fresh fruit and bacon. *Yield: 4 to 6 servings.*

 Wheat bran flakes are available at health food stores or in the flour aisle of grocery stores.

Swedish Pancakes

3 eggs, lightly beaten
3 tablespoons sugar
2 cups milk
3 tablespoons butter, melted
1/2 teaspoon salt
1 1/2 cups flour

Whisk the eggs, sugar, milk, melted butter and salt in a bowl. Whisk in the flour until smooth. Pour the batter 1/4 cup at a time onto a hot greased griddle. Cook until light brown on both sides, turning once. The pancakes will be thin, similar to crepes. Serve hot with butter and sprinkle with cinnamon and sugar. May also fill with fresh fruit and whipped cream or a sausage link and maple syrup; roll up to enclose. *Yield: 10 to 12 servings.*

Blueberry Coffee Cake

1 (2-layer) package butter recipe cake mix
8 ounces cream cheese, softened
$^1/_3$ cup vegetable oil
1 (16-ounce) can blueberries, drained
$^1/_2$ cup packed brown sugar
$^1/_2$ cup sugar
$2^1/_2$ tablespoons butter, melted
2 teaspoons cinnamon

Prepare the cake mix batter in a large mixing bowl according to the package directions; do not add water. Add the cream cheese and beat until well blended. Add the oil and beat well. Fold in the blueberries. Pour the batter into a greased 9×13-inch cake pan.

Combine the brown sugar, sugar, melted butter and cinnamon in a small bowl. Spoon the mixture over the top of the cake batter. Bake at 350 degrees for 50 to 55 minutes. *Yield: 15 servings.*

Cranberry Sour Cream Coffee Cake

Cake

1/2 cup (1 stick) butter or margarine,
    softened
1 cup sugar
2 eggs
2 cups flour
1 teaspoon baking powder
1 teaspoon baking soda
1/2 teaspoon salt
1 cup sour cream
1 teaspoon almond extract
1 (7-ounce) can whole cranberry sauce
1/2 cup chopped pecans

Sugar Icing

3/4 cup confectioners' sugar
1 tablespoon warm water
1/2 teaspoon almond extract

For the cake, Beat the butter and sugar in a large mixing bowl until light and fluffy. Add the eggs 1 at a time, beating well after each addition. Combine the flour, baking powder, baking soda and salt in a bowl. Add the flour mixture alternately with the sour cream to the butter mixture, ending with the sour cream and beating well after each addition. Add the almond extract and mix well. Pour a small amount of batter into a greased 10-inch tube pan. Swirl a small amount of cranberry sauce over the batter. Repeat this layering twice, ending with a cranberry swirl. Sprinkle with the pecans.

Bake at 350 degrees for 55 minutes. Let cool for 5 minutes before removing from the pan. Invert onto a serving plate.

For the icing, combine the confectioners' sugar, water and almond extract in a small bowl and mix until well blended. Drizzle the icing over the warm cake. *Yield: 16 servings.*

Sophie's Coffee Cake

This recipe came from Sophie's Cafeteria at the University of Tennessee.

Brown Sugar Topping
1/2 cup packed brown sugar
1 tablespoon flour
1 tablespoon cinnamon
1/4 teaspoon salt
1/4 cup chopped pecans
1/4 cup (1/2 stick) butter,
    cut into pieces

Cake
2 cups flour
2 teaspoons baking powder
1/2 cup plus 2 tablespoons sugar
3/4 teaspoon salt
1 egg, beaten
3/4 cup milk
1/2 cup shortening, melted

For the topping, combine the brown sugar, flour, cinnamon, salt and pecans in a small bowl. Cut in the butter until crumbly.

For the cake, combine the flour, baking powder, sugar and salt in a large mixing bowl. Add the egg and milk and mix just until moistened. Add the melted shortening and beat for 1 minute. Pour into a greased and floured 9-inch cake pan. Sprinkle the Brown Sugar Topping evenly over the cake batter. Bake at 400 degrees for 25 minutes. Yield: 8 to 10 servings.

Sour Cream Coffee Cake

3/4 cup (1 1/2 sticks) margarine, softened
1 1/2 cups sugar
1 cup sour cream
2 eggs
1 teaspoon vanilla extract
2 cups flour
1/2 teaspoon baking soda
1/2 teaspoon baking powder
3 tablespoons sugar
1 teaspoon cinnamon
3/4 cup finely chopped pecans (optional)

Beat the margarine and 1 1/2 cups sugar in a large mixing bowl until light and fluffy. Add the sour cream, eggs and vanilla and beat well. Combine the flour, baking soda and baking powder in a bowl. Add the flour mixture to the margarine mixture and beat until well blended. Combine 3 tablespoons sugar, cinnamon and pecans in a small bowl. Spoon half of the batter into a greased tube pan.

Sprinkle half of the cinnamon-sugar mixture over the cake batter. Repeat with the remaining cake batter and cinnamon-sugar mixture. Place in a cold oven and set the oven temperature to 325 degrees. Bake for 1 hour. Let cool in the pan for 5 minutes. Invert onto a serving plate. *Yield: 16 servings.*

Applesauce Muffins

1/2 cup (1 stick) butter or margarine, softened
1 1/2 cups sugar
2 eggs
2 cups flour
1 teaspoon baking powder
1 1/2 teaspoons cinnamon
1/2 teaspoon baking soda
1/4 teaspoon salt
1 1/4 cups applesauce

Beat the butter and sugar in a large mixing bowl until light and fluffy. Add the eggs 1 at a time, beating well after each addition. Combine the flour, baking powder, cinnamon, baking soda and salt in a separate bowl.

Add the flour mixture alternately with the applesauce to the creamed mixture, mixing well after each addition. Do not overbeat. Spoon the batter into greased muffin cups 2/3 full. Bake at 350 degrees for 20 to 25 minutes. Yield: 1 1/2 dozen muffins.

Oatmeal Blueberry Muffins

1 1/4 cups flour
1 cup quick-cooking oats
1/2 cup sugar
1 teaspoon baking powder
1/2 teaspoon baking soda
1/4 teaspoon salt
1 egg, beaten
1/2 cup water
1/2 cup vegetable oil
1 cup fresh blueberries
2 tablespoons sugar
1/4 teaspoon cinnamon

Combine the flour, oats, 1/2 cup sugar, baking powder, baking soda and salt in a large bowl. Combine the egg, water and oil in a separate bowl and mix well. Add the egg mixture to the flour mixture and mix well. Fold in the blueberries.

Spoon the batter into greased muffin cups 2/3 full. Combine 2 tablespoons sugar and cinnamon in a small bowl. Sprinkle over the batter in each muffin cup. Bake at 400 degrees for 18 to 20 minutes or until light brown. You may substitute thawed frozen blueberries for the fresh blueberries.
Yield: 1 dozen muffins.

Double-Orange Scones

2 cups flour
3 tablespoons sugar
2 1/2 teaspoons baking powder
2 teaspoons grated orange zest
1/3 cup cold butter, cut into pieces
1/2 cup chopped mandarin orange segments, drained
1/4 cup milk
1 egg, lightly beaten
1 tablespoon sugar

Combine the flour, 3 tablespoons sugar, baking powder and orange zest in a large bowl. Cut in the butter with a pastry blender until crumbly. Add the orange segments, milk and egg. Stir just until moistened; do not overmix. Knead the dough 10 times on a lightly floured surface.

Place the dough on a greased baking sheet. Shape into a 6-inch circle. Sprinkle with 1 tablespoon sugar. Cut the dough into 8 wedges and separate slightly. Bake at 400 degrees for 15 to 20 minutes or until light brown. Serve warm. *Yield: 8 scones.*

Crunchy Granola

7 cups rolled oats
1 cup wheat germ
1/2 cup unsweetened flaked coconut
1/2 cup sesame seeds
1/4 cup sunflower seed kernels
1 cup chopped almonds
1 cup chopped pecans

1 cup chopped dates
1 cup boiling water
1/2 cup corn oil
1/2 cup water
2 teaspoons vanilla extract
1 teaspoon salt
Confectioners' sugar (optional)

Combine the oats, wheat germ, coconut, sesame seeds, sunflower seed kernels, almonds and pecans in a large bowl; mix well and set aside. Cook the dates in 1 cup boiling water in a small saucepan until very soft. Pour into a blender container and process until very smooth. Combine the date mixture, corn oil, 1/2 cup water, vanilla and salt in a bowl and mix until well blended. Pour over the prepared oat mixture and mix until well coated. Rub with greased hands, breaking up large pieces. Spread onto greased baking sheets.

Bake at 225 degrees for 2 hours or until light brown, stirring often during baking. Let cool for a few minutes. May toss with a small amount of confectioners' sugar in a large sealable plastic bag if desired. Store in an airtight container. Serve as a snack or as a dry cereal with milk.
Yield: 11 cups (20 servings).

Brown's Breakfast

1 cup cran-grape juice
1 cup fresh orange juice
1/2 cup chopped unpeeled apple
1/2 banana, sliced
1/4 cup chopped pineapple

1/4 cup chopped unpeeled pear
1 (8-ounce) container vanilla yogurt
2 teaspoons blueberries
1/2 cup crushed ice

Combine the cran-grape juice, orange juice, apple, banana, pineapple, pear, yogurt, blueberries and ice in a blender container. Process for 1 minute or until of desired consistency. *Yield: 2 to 4 servings.*

Berry Smoothie

3/4 cup milk
1 (8-ounce) container vanilla yogurt
6 strawberries, hulled, sliced
1 cup frozen blackberries
4 ice cubes
1/4 cup sugar (optional)

Combine the milk, yogurt, strawberries, blackberries, ice cubes and sugar in a blender container. Process until smooth. *Yield: 1 serving.*

Apricot Nectar Hot Punch

1 (64-ounce) bottle apple juice
1 (64-ounce) bottle cranberry juice cocktail
1 (64-ounce) container orange juice
24 ounces apricot nectar
2 cups sugar

Combine the apple juice, cranberry juice, orange juice, apricot nectar and sugar in a large stockpot. Bring to a boil and simmer for 20 minutes, stirring occasionally. Serve hot. *Yield: 24 servings.*

Hot Cranberry Mull

1 1/2 quarts (48 ounces) cranberry juice cocktail
1 (64-ounce) can pineapple juice
1 1/2 cups water
1 cup packed brown sugar
1 tablespoon whole cloves
1 tablespoon whole allspice
4 to 5 cinnamon sticks
1/8 teaspoon nutmeg
1/8 teaspoon salt

Combine the cranberry juice, pineapple juice, water and brown sugar in a large stockpot. Combine the cloves, allspice and cinnamon sticks in a 6-inch cheesecloth square secured with string or a tea ball. Add to the stockpot. Stir in the nutmeg and salt. Bring to a boil and simmer over medium-low heat. Serve hot. *Yield: 20 servings.*

 For a delicious, healthy pick-me-up, try making a **Carrot Cooler.** *Combine 1/2 cup carrot juice with 1/2 cup pineapple juice. Serve over ice and garnish with a carrot curl.*

Hot Spiced Percolator Punch

9 cups pineapple juice
9 cups cranberry juice cocktail
4^1/$_2$ cups water
1 cup packed brown sugar
^{1}/$_2$ teaspoon whole cloves
4 cinnamon sticks, broken into small pieces
^{1}/$_4$ teaspoon salt (optional)

Combine the pineapple juice, cranberry juice, water and brown sugar in a
30-cup percolator. Combine the cloves, cinnamon sticks and salt and place
in the percolator basket. Perk according to the manufacturer's directions.
Serve hot. *Yield: 30 servings.*

Almond Punch

1 (48-ounce) can pineapple juice
1^1/$_2$ cups sugar
1 ounce almond extract
3 (6-ounce) cans frozen orange juice concentrate, thawed
3 (6-ounce) cans frozen lemonade concentrate, thawed

Combine the pineapple juice and sugar in a large container. Mix well,
stirring until the sugar is dissolved. Add the almond extract, orange juice
and lemonade concentrates. Add water according to the directions on the
cans of orange juice and lemonade. Mix until well blended. Chill until
serving time. *Yield: 24 to 30 servings.*

Pink Lady Punch

1 *quart (32 ounces) cranberry juice cocktail*
1 *quart (32 ounces) pineapple juice*
1 *cup sugar*
2 *quarts (64 ounces) ginger ale*

Combine the cranberry juice, pineapple juice and sugar in a large container. Mix well, stirring until the sugar is dissolved. Stir in the ginger ale immediately before serving. *Yield:* 1 *gallon (16 servings).*

Punch for a Crowd

3 *(3-ounce) packages strawberry gelatin*
7 *cups boiling water*
4 *cups sugar*
6 *cups cold water*
16 *ounces lemon juice*
2 *(64-ounce) cans pineapple juice*
3 *to 4 bottles ginger ale*

Combine the gelatin and boiling water in a large bowl. Add the sugar and mix well until the gelatin and sugar dissolve. Add the cold water, lemon juice and pineapple juice and mix well.

Freeze until about 2 hours before serving time. Let thaw for about 2 hours or until slushy. Place the mixture in a punch bowl. Stir in desired amount of ginger ale. Serve slushy. Adding more ginger ale will increase the number of servings. *Yield:* 50 *or more servings.*

Cranberry Tea

1 quart (32 ounces) cranberry juice cocktail
1 cup water
1 cup sugar
1/2 cup red hot cinnamon candies
1 cup orange juice
1 cup lemonade

Combine the cranberry juice, water and sugar in a large saucepan. Stir in the cinnamon candies. Cook over low heat until the sugar and candies dissolve, stirring occasionally. Stir in the orange juice and lemonade. Chill until serving time. Dilute with water to taste before serving. May serve warm or cold. Yield: 1 gallon tea concentrate.

Soups &
Salads

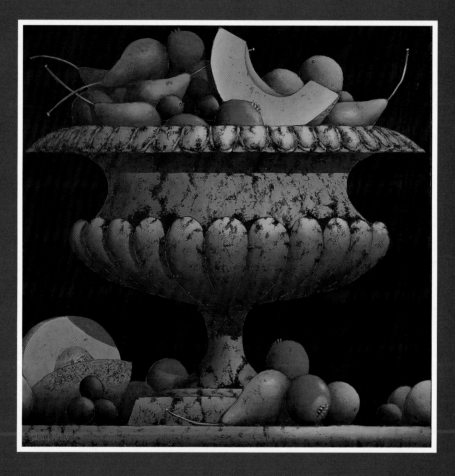

David Arms

David Arms, a self-taught artist, achieves a unique texture in his works through building multiple layers of paint, each time revealing fragments of the previous layers. A highlight of his technique is his unique use of color. For many years, David, of Nashville, Tennessee, has been a leading special event designer, producing award-winning corporate and social events from coast-to-coast. He says moving into painting was a natural transition since he has always "looked at an event as art and art as an event."

Shown on overleaf: *Urn with Fruit*

Gazpacho

1 (10-ounce) can beef bouillon
1 tablespoon olive oil
1/8 teaspoon Worcestershire sauce
1 tablespoon lemon juice
1 teaspoon basil
1 teaspoon salt
1 teaspoon pepper
6 cups tomato juice
1 onion, finely chopped
1 cup finely chopped celery
1 green bell pepper, finely chopped
4 tomatoes, peeled, chopped

Combine the beef bouillon, olive oil, Worcestershire sauce, lemon juice, basil, salt and pepper in a blender container. Process until well blended. Add the tomato juice and process. Pour into a large bowl and add the onion, celery, bell pepper and tomatoes; mix well.

Chill, covered, until serving time. Ladle into bowls to serve. Top with a spoonful of sour cream and sprinkle with chopped fresh chives. Serve with a sandwich for a delicious summertime meal. *Yield: 6 servings.*

Chilled Peach Soup

3 cardamom seeds
3 whole cloves
2 pounds peaches, peeled, chopped
2 cups orange juice
3 tablespoons lime juice
1/4 cup honey
1 1/2 teaspoons cinnamon
1 teaspoon ginger
1 (8-ounce) container vanilla yogurt
1 teaspoon finely chopped candied ginger

Place the cardamom seeds and whole cloves in a 6-inch square cheesecloth secured with a string. Combine the spice bag, peaches, orange juice, lime juice, honey, cinnamon and ginger in a large saucepan. Bring to a boil, reduce the heat and simmer for 10 minutes or until the peaches are tender, stirring occasionally.

Remove from the heat and discard the spice bag; let cool. Pour the mixture into a blender container. Process until smooth. Pour into a large bowl. Stir in the yogurt and candied ginger. Chill, covered, until serving time. Ladle into bowls to serve. Garnish with fresh peach slices and chopped fresh mint. Yield: 6 servings.

Potato Soup

6 potatoes, peeled, sliced
1 onion, chopped
1 rib celery, chopped
1 carrot, chopped
4 chicken bouillon cubes
1 tablespoon parsley flakes
5 cups water
1 teaspoon salt
1/4 teaspoon pepper
1/2 cup (1 stick) butter or margarine
1 (13-ounce) can evaporated milk

Combine the potatoes, onion, celery, carrot, bouillon cubes, parsley flakes, water, salt, pepper and butter in a large saucepan. Cook, covered, over low heat until the vegetables are tender. Remove the vegetables from the saucepan. Process the vegetables a small amount at a time in a blender. Return to the saucepan. Stir in the evaporated milk. Cook until heated through. *Yield: 8 to 10 servings.*

Cheese Soup

...ped onion
...s butter
...rrots, shredded
...tatoes, shredded
6 cups chicken broth
1/2 teaspoon thyme
1 bay leaf

1/8 teaspoon Tabasco sauce
1/2 teaspoon Worcestershire sauce
1/2 teaspoon sugar
Salt to taste
Pepper to taste
1 1/2 cups milk
1 to 2 cups shredded Cheddar cheese

Sauté the onion in the butter in a large saucepan until tender. Add the carrots, potatoes, chicken broth, thyme, bay leaf, Tabasco sauce, Worcestershire sauce, sugar, salt and pepper and mix well.

Simmer over medium heat until the potatoes and carrots are tender. Stir in the milk and cheese. Cook until the cheese melts, stirring until well blended. Simmer until heated through. Ladle into bowls to serve. *Yield: 6 to 8 servings.*

Tomato Basil Soup

4 cups tomato juice
4 cups crushed tomatoes
1 cup heavy cream

1/2 cup (1 stick) unsalted butter, softened
14 fresh basil leaves

Combine the tomato juice and crushed tomatoes in a saucepan. Simmer over medium heat for 30 minutes. Add the heavy cream, butter and basil leaves. Pour into a blender container. Process until well blended. Return to the saucepan and simmer over medium heat until heated through. Ladle into bowls to serve. Serve with warm, crusty bread. *Yield: 6 to 8 servings.*

Chicken Artichoke Soup

3 to 4 chicken breasts
1 package Uncle Ben's wild rice
1 white onion, chopped
2 tablespoons butter
1 to 2 tablespoons flour
1 (10-ounce) can chicken broth

1 (14-ounce) can artichoke hearts,
  quartered
Sliced mushrooms (optional)
1 pint half-and-half
1/4 cup chopped fresh parsley

Cook the chicken in boiling water to cover in a large stockpot until the chicken is cooked through and falls off the bone easily. Remove the chicken and let cool; reserving the stock. Cut the chicken into pieces, discarding the skin and bones. Cook the rice in the reserved chicken stock according to the package directions. Sauté the onion in the butter in a large saucepan until tender. Add the flour and cook until thickened, stirring constantly. Add the prepared rice, cooked chicken, chicken broth, artichoke hearts, mushrooms, half-and-half and parsley. Simmer for 30 minutes. Ladle into bowls to serve. *Yield: 4 to 6 servings.*

Homemade Chicken Noodle Soup

1 yellow onion, chopped
3 tablespoons olive oil
4 boneless skinless chicken breasts
4 cups (or more) water
4 to 5 medium carrots, sliced
4 medium ribs celery, sliced and leaves
  chopped

1 tablespoon (or less) salt
1 teaspoon sugar
1/4 teaspoon pepper
3 chicken bouillon cubes
8 ounces wide egg noodles

Sauté the onion in the olive oil in a large saucepan. Add the chicken, water, carrots, celery, salt, sugar, pepper and bouillon cubes. Bring to a boil, reduce the heat and cook, covered, until chicken is cooked through. Remove the chicken, reserving the stock and let cool. Cut into bite-size pieces. Return the chicken to the saucepan. Bring the chicken mixture to a boil and add the egg noodles. Cook until tender. Reduce the heat and simmer until heated through. Ladle into bowls to serve. This is great on a cold, winter night served with hot, crusty French bread. *Yield: 8 servings.*

Working Barn Stew

2 tablespoons olive oil
4 boneless skinless chicken breasts, cut into 1-inch pieces
1 cup chopped onion
1/2 green bell pepper, chopped
1/2 yellow bell pepper, chopped
1 teaspoon minced garlic
2 (14-ounce) cans stewed tomatoes
1 (15-ounce) can black beans, rinsed, drained
3/4 cup picante sauce
1 tablespoon chili powder
1 tablespoon cumin

Heat the olive oil in a large stockpot over medium heat. Add the chicken, onion, bell peppers and garlic and cook until the chicken is cooked through. Add the tomatoes, beans, picante sauce, chili powder and cumin.

Reduce the heat and simmer for 25 minutes or up to 2 hours. Ladle into bowls to serve. Top with shredded Cheddar cheese and sour cream. Serve with corn bread. *Yield: 6 servings.*

Téjas Chili

1 1/2 to 2 pounds ground beef
1/2 onion, chopped
2 (14-ounce) cans stewed tomatoes
2 (16-ounce) cans kidney beans
2 (10-ounce) cans tomato soup
2 to 3 cups water
3 tablespoons prepared mustard
1/2 cup pickle juice
1/4 cup honey
1 tablespoon salt
1 teaspoon pepper
4 to 5 pinches chili powder
4 to 5 pinches cilantro
4 to 5 pinches cumin

Brown the ground beef with the onion in a large skillet, stirring until the ground beef is crumbly; drain. Spoon the ground beef and onion into a large stockpot. Add the tomatoes, beans, tomato soup, water, mustard, pickle juice, honey, salt, pepper, chili powder, cilantro and cumin and mix well. Cook over low heat for 1 hour. Ladle into bowls to serve.
Yield: 12 to 16 servings.

Chili for a Crowd

5 pounds ground beef
4 (10-ounce) cans beef bouillon
1 tablespoon pepper
1 tablespoon chili powder
1 tablespoon cumin
1/2 teaspoon garlic powder
1/2 teaspoon onion powder
2 (6-ounce) cans tomato paste
Salt to taste
Sugar to taste
2 (29-ounce) cans kidney beans, drained

Brown the ground beef in a stockpot, stirring until crumbly; drain. Add the beef bouillon, pepper, chili powder, cumin, garlic powder, onion powder and tomato paste. Simmer for 45 minutes. Stir in the salt and sugar to taste. Add water for desired consistency. Spoon the beans into bowls. Ladle the chili over the beans. Yield: 20 servings.

Asparagus Salad

3 pounds fresh asparagus
2 (14-ounce) cans hearts of palm,
    drained, cut into 1/2-inch pieces
2 cups cherry tomatoes
3/4 cup vegetable oil

1/2 cup cider vinegar
1 1/2 teaspoons salt
1 teaspoon pepper
1 1/2 teaspoons minced garlic

Trim the asparagus. Steam for 4 to 5 minutes or until tender-crisp. Rinse in cold water; drain. Combine the asparagus, hearts of palm and tomatoes in a large sealable plastic bag. Combine the oil, vinegar, salt, pepper and garlic in a bowl and mix well.

Pour the dressing over the vegetables in the plastic bag. Marinate, in the refrigerator, for 8 hours; turning the bag occasionally. Drain the vegetables and serve on a bed of lettuce. Yield: 8 to 10 servings.

Broccoli and Bacon Salad

1 cup chopped green onions
1 cup mayonnaise
1 cup raisins
1/2 cup sugar

1/4 cup cider vinegar
2 bunches broccoli, chopped
1 pound bacon, crisp-cooked, crumbled

Combine the green onions, mayonnaise, raisins, sugar and vinegar in a bowl and mix well. Chill, covered, for 1 hour or more. Add the broccoli and bacon immediately before serving and toss to mix well. Yield: 8 to 10 servings.

Tri-Colored Vegetable Pasta Salad

Dressing
1/2 cup white balsamic vinegar
1/2 cup extra-virgin olive oil
3 to 4 tablespoons honey
1/4 cup Dijon mustard
1/4 cup prepared Italian salad
    dressing

Salad
1 1/2 cups broccoli florets
1 1/2 cups baby carrots
1 1/2 cups cauliflower florets
16 ounces tri-colored rotini, cooked
1 cup grated Parmesan or Romano
    cheese
White pepper to taste (optional)
Salt to taste (optional)

For *the dressing*, combine the vinegar, olive oil, honey, mustard and Italian dressing in a jar with a tight-fitting lid. Shake vigorously to mix well. Chill until serving time.

For *the salad*, steam the broccoli, carrots and cauliflower for a few minutes or until tender-crisp; rinse with cold water and drain. Combine the broccoli, carrots and cauliflower in a food processor container. Process until finely chopped. Combine the pasta and vegetables in a large bowl.

Pour desired amount of dressing over the salad immediately before serving and toss to mix well. Stir in the Parmesan cheese, pepper and salt. The pasta will absorb the dressing if stored overnight. You may toss with more dressing before serving again if desired. *Yield: 8 servings.*

The Best Chicken Pasta Salad

16 ounces angel hair pasta
2 tablespoons olive oil
2 tablespoons salt
1/2 teaspoon pepper
4 teaspoons red wine vinegar
1/2 to 3/4 cup olive oil
1/4 cup Dijon mustard
1 cup mayonnaise
1/4 cup prepared vinaigrette dressing

1/4 cup chopped fresh parsley
1/4 cup chopped green onions
1 to 2 tablespoons basil
1 garlic clove, minced
Salt to taste
Pepper or lemon pepper to taste
6 boneless skinless chicken breasts,
   cooked, chopped
Freshly grated Parmesan cheese

Cook the pasta al dente using the package directions and adding
2 tablespoons olive oil to the cooking water; rinse and drain. Combine
the cooked pasta, 2 tablespoons salt, 1/2 teaspoon pepper, red wine vinegar,
and 1/2 cup olive oil in a large bowl.

Marinate, covered, in the refrigerator for 8 to 10 hours. Combine the
mustard, mayonnaise, vinaigrette dressing, parsley, green onions, basil,
garlic, salt and pepper to taste in a bowl and mix well. Stir into the pasta
mixture. Fold in the chicken. Top with the Parmesan cheese. You may
also add olives, artichokes or omit the chicken. This salad is easy to vary
according to taste. *Yield: 12 servings*.

Festive Fruit Salad

Fruit Salad Dressing
3 ounces cream cheese, softened
1/2 cup confectioners' sugar
2 teaspoons lemon juice
8 ounces whipped topping

Salad
1 medium pineapple, peeled, cored, chopped
1 Red Delicious apple, chopped
1 Golden Delicious apple, chopped
1 Granny Smith apple, chopped
1 small cantaloupe, chopped
1 pint strawberries, hulled, sliced
1 pint blueberries
4 cups mixed red and green seedless grapes
3 kiwifruit, peeled, sliced
1 large firm banana, sliced

For the dressing, beat the cream cheese in a mixing bowl until light. Add the confectioners' sugar and lemon juice and beat until smooth. Fold in the whipped topping. Chill until serving time.

For the salad, combine the pineapple, apples, cantaloupe, strawberries, blueberries, grapes, kiwifruit and banana in a large, clear, glass bowl. Spread the dressing evenly over the fruit. You may layer the fruit if desired. Garnish with additional berries. *Yield: 16 to 20 servings.*

Honey Fruit Compote

1 (20-ounce) can pineapple chunks
2 (11-ounce) cans mandarin oranges, drained
1 1/2 cups mixed red and green seedless grapes, halved
3 kiwifruit, peeled, sliced
1/2 cup orange juice
1/4 cup honey
1 tablespoon lemon juice

Drain the pineapple, reserving the juice. Combine the pineapple, mandarin oranges, grapes and kiwifruit in a large, clear, glass bowl. Combine the reserved pineapple juice, orange juice, honey and lemon juice in a bowl and mix well. Pour over the fruit, tossing to mix well. Chill, covered, until serving time. *Yield: 6 to 8 servings.*

Apricot Salad

2 (3-ounce) packages apricot gelatin
2 cups boiling water
1 1/2 cups apricot nectar
1 cup chopped pecans
1 cup maraschino cherries, chopped
1/2 cup crushed pineapple, reserving 1/2 cup juice
2 bananas, chopped
1 egg
1/2 cup sugar
2 tablespoons flour
2 tablespoons melted butter
3 ounces cream cheese, softened
8 ounces whipped topping

Dissolve the gelatin in the boiling water in a bowl. Stir in the apricot nectar. Chill until partially set. Stir in the pecans, cherries, pineapple and bananas. Pour into a 9×13-inch dish. Chill, covered, until set.

Beat the egg and sugar in a mixing bowl until thickened and pale yellow. Combine the egg mixture, flour and melted butter in a small saucepan. Add the reserved pineapple juice and cook over medium heat until thickened. Remove from the heat. Add the cream cheese and beat until smooth. Let cool. Fold in the whipped topping. Spread the topping mixture over the apricot salad. Chill, covered, until serving time. *Yield: 8 to 12 servings.*

Romaine and Noodle Salad

Red Wine Vinaigrette
2/3 cup sugar
1/3 cup red wine vinegar
1/4 teaspoon garlic powder
1/4 teaspoon pepper
1 cup olive oil

Salad
2 (3-ounce) packages chicken-flavored
  ramen noodles, broken
3 tablespoons margarine
1/3 cup sesame seeds
1 head napa cabbage, thinly sliced
1 head romaine, thinly sliced
1 red bell pepper, finely chopped
4 green onions, finely chopped
1/2 cup slivered almonds

For the vinaigrette, combine the sugar, red wine vinegar, garlic powder and pepper in a blender container. Process until well blended. Add the olive oil in a fine stream, processing constantly until smooth. Chill until serving time.

For the salad, sauté the ramen noodles in the margarine in a skillet. Add the seasoning packet from the ramen noodles and the sesame seeds; mix well. Remove from the heat and let cool. Combine the cabbage, lettuce, ramen noodle mixture, bell pepper, green onions and almonds in a salad bowl. Pour the vinaigrette over the salad immediately before serving and toss to mix well. Yield: 8 servings.

Winter Fruit Salad with
Lemon Poppy Seed Dressing

Dressing
1/2 cup sugar
1/3 cup lemon juice
2 teaspoons finely chopped onion
1 teaspoon Dijon mustard
1/2 teaspoon salt
2/3 cup vegetable oil
1 tablespoon poppy seeds

Salad
1 large head romaine
4 ounces (1 cup) shredded Swiss cheese
1 cup cashews, broken into pieces
1/4 cup craisins
1 apple, chopped
1 pear, chopped

For *the dressing*, combine the sugar, lemon juice, onion, mustard and salt in a blender container. Process until well blended. Add the oil in a fine stream, processing constantly until smooth. Add the poppy seeds and process for a few seconds to mix well. Chill until serving time.

For *the salad*, tear the lettuce into bite-size pieces into a large bowl. Add the Swiss cheese, cashews, craisins, apple and pear and toss to mix well. Pour the desired amount of dressing over the salad immediately before serving and toss to mix well. *Yield: 6 to 8 servings*.

Spinach and Strawberry Salad

Cider Vinaigrette
1/2 cup vegetable oil
1/2 cup sugar
1/4 cup cider vinegar
2 tablespoons toasted sesame seeds
1 tablespoon poppy seeds
1 1/2 teaspoons minced fresh onion
1/4 teaspoon Worcestershire sauce
1/4 teaspoon paprika

Salad
Fresh spinach
Fresh strawberries, hulled, sliced
Fresh sliced mushrooms (optional)
Toasted almond slices (optional)

For the vinaigrette, combine the oil, sugar, cider vinegar, sesame seeds, poppy seeds, onion, Worcestershire sauce and paprika in a jar with a tight-fitting lid. Shake vigorously to mix well. Chill until serving time.

For the salad, rinse the spinach and spin dry. Tear into bite-size pieces, discarding the stems. Combine the spinach, strawberries, mushrooms and almonds in a salad bowl. Pour desired amount of the vinaigrette over the salad immediately before serving and toss to mix well. *Yield: Variable.*

with Raspberry Vinaigrette

Salad
2 bunches Bibb or Boston lettuce
1 bunch red leaf lettuce
8 ounces Monterey Jack cheese, cubed
1 bunch seedless red grapes, halved
1 cup toasted pecans or almonds
   (optional)

For *the vinaigrette*, combine the vinegar, sugar, onion, jam, dry mustard and salt in a blender container. Process until well blended. Add the olive oil in a fine stream, processing constantly until smooth. Chill until serving time.

For *the salad*, rinse the lettuces and spin dry. Tear into bite-size pieces. Combine the lettuce, cheese, grapes and almonds in a large salad bowl. Pour the desired amount of vinaigrette over the salad immediately before serving and toss to mix well. *Yield: 6 to 8 servings.*

Balsamic Vinaigrette

1/4 cup balsamic vinegar
1/4 cup orange juice
1/4 cup olive oil
2 tablespoons chopped fresh basil
1 tablespoon honey mustard
1 garlic clove, minced (optional)
Salt to taste
Pepper to taste

Whisk the vinegar, orange juice, olive oil, basil, honey mustard, garlic, salt and pepper in a bowl. Pour into a jar with a tight-fitting lid. Shake vigorously to mix well. Chill until serving time.

This dressing is delicious on a green salad topped with chopped red bell pepper, chopped green apple and grated Parmesan cheese. *Yield: 6 servings.*

Vegetables & Side Dishes

Debbie Wingo

Debbie Wingo describes her work as passionate, sincere, and creative. She says each piece she creates is "inspired by a deep inner search for the pure happiness life has to offer." Debbie, from Nashville, Tennessee, studied art at the University of Tennessee and Watkins Institute in Nashville. She calls her paintings an expression of "what I discover in my daily life. The work is a gift from God and I want to share it with you."

Shown on overleaf: *Peppers*

Green Beans in Sweet Vinaigrette

1 tablespoon plus 1 teaspoon red currant jelly
1 tablespoon cider vinegar or white balsamic vinegar
¹/₈ teaspoon dry mustard
¹/₈ teaspoon salt
1 pound fresh green beans, trimmed, strings removed
¹/₄ cup finely chopped red bell pepper

Combine the red currant jelly, vinegar, mustard and salt in a small saucepan. Cook over low heat until the mixture is well blended, stirring constantly. Set aside.

Steam the green beans for 10 minutes or until tender-crisp. Steam the bell pepper for 1 minute or until tender-crisp. Pour the jelly mixture over the green beans and bell pepper in a serving dish and toss to mix well. Serve immediately. *Yield: 4 to 6 servings.*

 When purchasing fresh green beans, only buy those that have a slender shape and a crisp feel. Store in a sealable plastic bag in the refrigerator for no more than 2 days after purchasing.

Fourth of July Bean Casserole

1/2 pound ground beef
1/2 pound bacon, chopped
1 cup chopped onion
1 (28-ounce) can pork and beans
1 (17-ounce) can lima beans, rinsed, drained
1 (15-ounce) can kidney beans, rinsed, drained
1/2 cup barbecue sauce
1/2 cup ketchup
1/2 cup sugar
1/2 cup packed brown sugar
2 tablespoons prepared mustard
2 tablespoons molasses

Brown the ground beef in a skillet with the bacon and onion, stirring until the ground beef is crumbly and the bacon is crisp; drain. Spoon into a 2 1/2-quart baking dish. Add the pork and beans, lima beans and kidney beans.

Combine the barbecue sauce, ketchup, sugar, brown sugar, mustard and molasses in a small bowl and mix well. Stir into the bean mixture. Bake, covered, at 350 degrees for 45 minutes. Uncover and bake for 15 minutes longer. *Yield: 12 servings*.

Broccoli Casserole

8 ounces cream cheese
1 1/4 cups milk
2 tablespoons butter
2 tablespoons flour

2 (10-ounce) packages frozen chopped
  broccoli
Shredded Cheddar cheese
Crushed Cheddar goldfish crackers

Combine the cream cheese, milk, butter and flour in a double boiler. Cook until the cream cheese is melted and the mixture is creamy, stirring constantly. Pour into a greased 2-quart baking dish. Cook the broccoli according to the package directions; drain. Add to the cream cheese mixture and mix well. Top with Cheddar cheese to taste and cover with crushed goldfish crackers. Bake at 350 degrees for 35 to 40 minutes or until bubbly. Yield: 6 to 8 servings.

Copper Pennies

1 (10-ounce) can tomato soup
1/2 cup white vinegar
1 cup sugar
1 small onion, chopped
1 green bell pepper, chopped

1 teaspoon prepared mustard
1 teaspoon Worcestershire sauce
Salt to taste
Pepper to taste
2 pounds carrots, sliced

Combine the soup, vinegar, sugar, onion, bell pepper, mustard, Worcestershire sauce, salt and pepper in a bowl and mix well. Cook the carrots in boiling water to cover in a large saucepan until tender; drain. Pour the soup mixture over the warm carrots. Marinate, covered, in the refrigerator for 8 to 10 hours. Drain and serve cold. You may also heat and serve warm. Yield: 12 servings.

...berry Salsa

...n or frozen cranberries, thawed
...2 purple onion, chopped
...apeño chiles, seeded, chopped
...2 cup chopped fresh cilantro
$^1/_2$ cup honey
2 tablespoons fresh lime juice
1 tablespoon grated orange zest

...onion, jalapeño chiles, cilantro, honey, lime juice and orange... od processor, pulsing 6 to 8 times or until coarsely chopped; scrape the ...ide occasionally. Chill, covered, for 8 hours before serving. Yield: 2$^1/_2$ cups.

Amish Corn

1 (16-ounce) can whole kernel corn
1 (16-ounce) can cream-style corn
2 eggs, beaten
1 cup sour cream
$^2/_3$ cup margarine, melted
1 (9-ounce) package Jiffy corn muffin mix

Combine the whole kernel corn, cream-style corn, eggs, sour cream, melted margarine and corn muffin mix in a large bowl and mix well. Pour into a greased 9×13-inch baking dish. Bake at 350 degrees for 30 to 35 minutes. Yield: 10 to 12 servings.

Sautéed Fresh Mushrooms

2 pounds fresh mushrooms, sliced
1/4 cup Worcestershire sauce
6 tablespoons butter
1/3 (5-ounce) bottle soy sauce
Dash of white cooking wine

Garlic salt to taste
Salt to taste
Pepper to taste
3 tablespoons honey

Combine the mushrooms, Worcestershire sauce, butter, soy sauce, cooking wine, garlic salt, salt and pepper in a large skillet. Cook over low heat for 30 minutes, stirring occasionally. Add the honey and cook, covered, for 30 minutes longer. Serve hot as a side dish or over chicken or steak. Yield: 4 to 6 servings.

Roasted Wild Mushrooms

8 garlic cloves, thinly sliced
3 tablespoons olive oil
3 tablespoons balsamic or red wine
    vinegar
3 sprigs fresh rosemary, chopped

3 sprigs fresh thyme, chopped
1 pound fresh wild mushrooms
    (shiitake, oyster, cremini)
1/4 teaspoon salt
1/8 teaspoon freshly ground pepper

Line a large baking sheet with foil. Combine the garlic, olive oil, vinegar, rosemary and thyme in a large bowl. Add the mushrooms and toss to coat well. Add the salt and pepper and mix well.

Spread in a single layer on the prepared baking sheet. Roast at 425 degrees for 25 minutes or until the mushrooms look crisp around the edges. Spoon into a serving bowl and serve immediately. Yield: 4 servings.

Mushroom Casserole

1 cup toasted bread crumbs
2 tablespoons margarine
3 pounds fresh mushrooms
1/2 cup chopped onion
1/2 cup chopped celery
1 teaspoon salt
1/2 teaspoon pepper
1/2 cup mayonnaise
2 eggs, beaten
1 1/2 cups milk
1 (10-ounce) can cream of mushroom soup
1 cup shredded Cheddar cheese

Sprinkle the bread crumbs over the bottom of a 2-quart baking dish. Melt the margarine in a saucepan. Sauté the mushrooms, onion and celery in the margarine until tender. Add the salt and pepper. Stir in the mayonnaise. Pour the mushroom mixture over the bread crumbs.

Combine the eggs, milk and soup in a small bowl. Pour over the mushroom mixture. Bake at 325 degrees for 50 minutes. Top with the cheese. Bake for 10 minutes longer. *Yield: 8 servings.*

Baked Sweet Onions

4 large sweet onions
4 (12-inch) squares of foil
¼ cup (½ stick) butter, cut into 4 tablespoons
Salt to taste
Pepper to taste
½ cup grated Parmesan cheese

Cut the onions into quarters; do not cut all the way through. Place 1 onion on each square of foil. Place 1 tablespoon butter in each onion. Sprinkle with salt and pepper. Top each onion with 2 tablespoons Parmesan cheese. Wrap the onions in the foil; do not seal the top of the foil. Place the onion packets on a baking sheet. Bake at 400 degrees for 1 hour. Unwrap and serve hot. *Yield: 4 servings.*

Baby Red Potatoes

2 pounds baby red potatoes, cut into halves
Olive oil
Fresh or dried dill to taste
Salt to taste
Pepper to taste

Place the potatoes on a foil-lined baking sheet. Brush generously with olive oil. Sprinkle with the dill. Bake at 375 degrees for 30 minutes or until tender. Season with salt and pepper. *Yield: 4 to 6 servings.*

Parmesan Potatoes

6 tablespoons butter or margarine, melted
3 tablespoons grated Parmesan cheese
8 medium red potatoes, halved

Pour the melted butter into a 9×13-inch baking pan. Sprinkle the Parmesan cheese over the melted butter. Arrange the potatoes, cut side down, over the cheese. Bake at 400 degrees for 40 to 45 minutes or until tender. *Yield: 4 or 5 servings.*

Potatoes Provençal

2 pounds red potatoes, sliced
   1/3 inch thick
4 garlic cloves, minced
2 medium red onions, thinly sliced
3 tablespoons olive oil
3 tablespoons chopped fresh basil

Pepper to taste
1 teaspoon tamari
4 tomatoes, thinly sliced
1/2 cup sliced black olives
1 cup grated Parmesan cheese

Steam the potatoes until tender-crisp; drain. Sauté the garlic and onions in the olive oil in a skillet until tender. Combine the potatoes, garlic, onions basil, pepper and tamari in a bowl and mix well.

Place half of the potato mixture in a greased 2-quart baking dish. Cover with half of the tomatoes, olives and Parmesan cheese. Repeat the layers. Bake, loosely covered with foil, at 350 degrees for 30 minutes. Uncover and bake 20 minutes longer. *Yield: 6 to 8 servings.*

Twice-Baked Potatoes

4 (10-ounce) baking potatoes
Vegetable oil
1/2 cup sour cream
1/4 cup (1/2 stick) butter or margarine, softened
1/4 cup milk
2 tablespoons chopped green onions
1/2 teaspoon salt
1/8 teaspoon pepper
4 slices bacon, crisp-cooked, crumbled
1/2 cup shredded Cheddar cheese

Coat the potatoes with the oil. Bake at 400 degrees for 1 hour or until soft. Let cool. Cut a 1-inch strip lengthwise on each potato. Scoop out the potato pulp carefully into a mixing bowl, reserving potato skin shells. Add the sour cream, butter, milk, green onions, salt, pepper and bacon. Beat at medium speed until well mixed and the potato mixture is smooth.

Spoon the potato mixture into the potato skin shells. Place the stuffed potatoes on a baking sheet. Bake at 350 degrees for 15 minutes. Top each potato with cheese. Bake for 5 minutes longer or until the cheese is melted. Yield: 4 servings.

Scrumptious Potatoes

1 (32-ounce) package frozen hash
   brown potatoes, thawed
2 (10-ounce) cans cream of chicken
   soup
1 cup sour cream
1/2 cup shredded Cheddar cheese
1/2 cup chopped onion

1/2 cup milk
1 tablespoon parsley flakes
2 teaspoons salt
1/8 teaspoon garlic powder
1/2 cup (1 stick) butter, melted
Crushed cornflakes

Combine the hash brown potatoes, soup, sour cream, cheese, onion, milk, parsley, salt and garlic powder in a large bowl and mix well. Spoon into a greased 9×13-inch baking dish. Combine the melted butter and cornflakes in a small bowl and mix well. Spread evenly over the top. Bake at 350 degrees for 1 hour. Yield: 12 servings.

Holiday Sweet Potatoes

6 cups mashed cooked sweet potatoes
1 1/2 cups sugar
4 eggs
1 cup (2 sticks) butter, melted
2 teaspoons vanilla extract

1 1/2 cups packed brown sugar
1 1/2 cups chopped pecans or walnuts
1/2 cup flour
1/2 cup (1 stick) butter

Combine the sweet potatoes, sugar, eggs, 1 cup melted butter and vanilla in a mixing bowl and beat until smooth. Spoon into a 9×13-inch baking dish. Combine the brown sugar, pecans, flour and 1/2 cup butter in a small bowl and mix until crumbly. Spread on top of the sweet potato mixture. Bake at 350 degrees for 40 minutes or until set. Yield: 12 servings.

Spinach Cabrinee

1/4 cup chopped onion
1 tablespoon butter
2 (10-ounce) packages frozen spinach,
    cooked, drained
4 cups shredded Monterey Jack cheese
2 cups sour cream

1/2 cup (1 stick) butter, melted
1/4 cup sliced mushrooms
1/4 teaspoon salt
1/4 teaspoon pepper
1/8 teaspoon oregano

Sauté the onion in 1 tablespoon butter in a skillet until golden brown. Combine the spinach, cheese, sour cream, 1/2 cup melted butter, mushrooms, sautéed onion, salt, pepper and oregano in a large bowl and mix well. Spoon into a greased 9×13-inch baking dish. Bake at 325 degrees for 45 minutes. *Yield: 10 servings.*

Spinach Artichoke Casserole

11 ounces cream cheese, softened
1/2 cup (1 stick) butter, melted
3 teaspoons lemon juice
1 teaspoon seasoned salt

4 (10-ounce) packages frozen spinach,
    cooked, drained
2 (14-ounce) cans artichoke hearts,
    drained, quartered

Combine the cream cheese, melted butter, lemon juice and seasoned salt in a bowl and mix well. Add the spinach and mix well. Place the artichoke hearts in a 9×13-inch baking dish. Spoon the spinach mixture over the artichoke hearts. Cover with foil. Pierce holes in the foil with a fork to allow steam to escape. Bake at 350 degrees for 30 minutes. *Yield: 10 to 12 servings.*

Squash Casserole

2 pounds squash, sliced, cooked, drained
1 onion, finely chopped
1/4 cup (1/2 stick) margarine, melted
1/4 cup evaporated milk
2 eggs, beaten
1 teaspoon (or less) sugar
Salt to taste
Pepper to taste
2 cups shredded sharp Cheddar cheese
1/2 (2-ounce) package slivered almonds, toasted
10 saltine crackers, crushed
1/4 cup (1/2 stick) margarine, melted

Combine the cooked squash, onion, 1/4 cup melted margarine, evaporated milk, eggs, sugar, salt and pepper in a bowl and mix well. Combine the Cheddar cheese and almonds in a small bowl and mix well. Layer the squash mixture and the cheese mixture in a greased 9×13-inch baking dish.

Sprinkle the crushed crackers over the top of the squash mixture. Pour 1/4 cup melted margarine over the crackers. Bake at 350 degrees for 30 minutes or until bubbly. *Yield: 6 to 8 servings.*

Summer Tomato Tart

1 (1-crust) pie pastry
2 cups shredded mozzarella cheese
2 1/2 tablespoons chopped fresh basil
4 to 5 ripe tomatoes, cut into 1/2-inch slices
3/4 teaspoon salt
1/2 teaspoon freshly ground pepper
1/4 cup virgin olive oil

Press the pie pastry into a 10-inch springform tart pan. Sprinkle the cheese into the prepared pan. Sprinkle the basil on top of the cheese. Arrange the tomato slices evenly over the top. Sprinkle with the salt and pepper. Drizzle the olive oil over the top. Bake at 400 degrees for 30 minutes. Remove the side of the pan. Slice into wedges and serve warm. Yield: 8 *servings*.

Baked Zucchini with Parmesan and Prosciutto

3 small zucchini
1/4 pound thinly sliced prosciutto
1 tablespoon chopped fresh oregano
1/4 cup freshly grated Parmesan cheese
Freshly ground pepper
1 tablespoon melted butter or olive oil

Cook the zucchini in boiling water to cover in a saucepan for 5 minutes or until tender-crisp. Rinse in cool water and drain. Slice the zucchini lengthwise into quarters. Wrap each piece of zucchini with a slice of prosciutto. Place side by side in a greased baking dish. Sprinkle with the oregano, cheese and pepper. Drizzle with the butter. Bake at 400 degrees for 10 to 15 minutes. Yield: 4 *servings*.

Curried Orange Rice

¹/₄ cup (¹/₂ stick) butter
1 medium onion, thinly sliced
1 teaspoon curry powder
1 cup uncooked white rice
1 cup orange juice
1 cup chicken broth
¹/₂ cup golden raisins
1 teaspoon salt
1 bay leaf

Melt the butter in a heavy saucepan. Add the onion and sauté until tender. Stir in the curry powder and the rice. Cook for 2 minutes, stirring constantly. Add the orange juice, chicken broth, raisins, salt and bay leaf.

Bring to a boil and reduce the heat. Simmer, covered, for 15 to 20 minutes or until the liquid is absorbed and the rice is tender. Remove the bay leaf before serving. *Yield: 6 to 8 servings.*

Old-Fashioned Dressing

2 eggs, beaten
2 cups buttermilk
2 cups chopped celery
1 cup chopped onion
2 1/2 cups self-rising flour
1 1/2 cups self-rising cornmeal
2 teaspoons salt
1/2 cup (1 stick) butter, melted
3 to 4 cups chicken broth
1 egg, beaten
Pepper to taste

Combine 2 eggs, buttermilk, celery and onion in a bowl. Combine the flour, cornmeal and salt in a large bowl. Add the egg mixture and mix well. Pour into a greased cast-iron skillet.

Bake at 350 degrees for 45 to 60 minutes. Let cool. Invert and wrap in plastic wrap. Let stand at room temperature for 2 to 3 days. Crumble the corn bread into a large bowl. Add the melted butter, chicken broth, 1 egg and pepper; mix well. Pour into a 9×13-inch baking dish. Bake at 350 degrees for 1 hour. *Yield: 10 to 12 servings.*

Pasta with Lemon Cream Sauce

1 cup heavy cream
2 tablespoons chopped fresh parsley
2 teaspoons grated lemon zest
$^1/_2$ teaspoon salt
2 tablespoons butter
2 tablespoons grated Parmesan cheese
4 cups hot cooked pasta

Heat the cream in a large skillet over medium heat until thickened and bubbly. Add the parsley, lemon zest and salt. Cook for 30 seconds, stirring constantly. Reduce the heat to low and add the butter, Parmesan cheese and pasta. Toss to coat well and serve immediately. This is an easy, elegant side dish that is great served with a grilled steak. Yield: 4 *servings*.

Penne with Tomato Cream Sauce

1 (14-ounce) can diced tomatoes
$^1/_2$ cup heavy cream
2 garlic cloves, minced
$^3/_4$ teaspoon tarragon or basil
Salt to taste
Sugar to taste
8 ounces penne pasta, cooked
Freshly grated Parmesan cheese

Combine the tomatoes, cream, garlic, tarragon, salt and sugar in a saucepan. Bring to a boil and reduce the heat. Simmer for 20 to 30 minutes or until thickened, stirring occasionally. Serve over the hot cooked pasta and top with Parmesan cheese. Yield: 2 *to 4 servings*.

Entrées

Tricia Hastings

Tricia Hastings of Nashville, Tennessee, says she challenges herself as a painter to create work that is strong, distinct, and captivating. Her subject matter ranges from a pair of running shoes tossed on an oriental rug to vignettes of European life. The "ordinary and extraordinary" scenes she interprets "become a joy to transform into my vision of beauty." Tricia says she hopes to create harmonious, intense pieces that command one's attention. From Knoxville, Tennessee, Tricia studied art at the University of Tennessee.

Shown on overleaf: *El Cordobes*

Beef Tenderloin

1/2 cup red wine
1/4 cup Worcestershire sauce
2 tablespoons minced garlic
2 tablespoons olive oil
Freshly ground pepper to taste
1 (3- to 4-pound) beef tenderloin

Combine the wine, Worcestershire sauce, garlic, olive oil and pepper in a bowl and mix well. Pour over the beef tenderloin in a glass dish. Marinate, covered, in the refrigerator for 8 to 10 hours. Place the tenderloin in a roasting pan; discard the marinade. Bake at 500 degrees for 5 minutes per pound. Turn off the oven and leave the tenderloin in the oven for 2 hours; do not open the oven. Slice before serving. Yield: 8 to 12 servings.

Three-Day Brisket

6 pounds lean brisket
2 teaspoons meat tenderizer
1 (4-ounce) bottle liquid smoke
1/3 bottle Worcestershire sauce
Seasoned salt
Celery salt
Garlic salt
Pepper

Sprinkle each side of the brisket with the meat tenderizer. Place the brisket in a large roasting pan. Pour the liquid smoke and Worcestershire sauce over the brisket. Sprinkle with the seasoned salt, celery salt, garlic salt and pepper. Marinate in the refrigerator for 8 to 10 hours, basting occasionally. Bake, tightly covered, at 250 degrees for 7 hours. Let cool and chill, covered, for 8 to 10 hours; reserving the sauce. Slice the brisket into strips. Heat the brisket and reserved sauce and serve warm. Yield: 16 servings.

Barbecue Flank Steak

1 (1½- to 2-pound) flank steak
¾ cup vegetable oil
¼ cup soy sauce
1 bunch green onions, chopped
3 tablespoons honey
2 tablespoons vinegar
1½ teaspoons garlic powder
1½ teaspoons ginger

Pierce the flank steak with a fork. Place in a glass dish. Combine the oil, soy sauce, green onions, honey, vinegar, garlic powder and ginger in a small bowl and mix well. Pour over the flank steak.

Marinate, covered, in the refrigerator for 8 to 10 hours. Drain the marinade and discard. Grill over hot coals for 8 to 10 minutes on each side for medium-rare. Slice diagonally into thin strips to serve. Serve with pasta and a Caesar salad. *Yield: 4 servings.*

Chinese Pepper Steak

2 tablespoons vegetable oil
1 teaspoon salt
1 teaspoon ginger
1/4 teaspoon pepper
1 garlic clove, minced
1 1/2 pounds round steak, cut into
   thin strips
2 onions, sliced

2 green bell peppers, sliced
1 (8-ounce) can sliced water chestnuts
1 (4-ounce) can sliced mushrooms
1/2 cup beef bouillon
1/4 cup soy sauce
1 teaspoon sugar
1 tablespoon cornstarch
1/4 cup water

Heat the oil, salt, ginger, pepper and garlic in a skillet. Brown the steak in the hot oil mixture. Remove the steak from the skillet and keep warm. Sauté the onions, bell peppers, water chestnuts and mushrooms in the skillet until tender-crisp. Return the steak to the skillet and add the beef bouillon, soy sauce, sugar, cornstarch and water.

Simmer until thickened, stirring occasionally. Serve over hot cooked rice. You may substitute chicken strips for the steak and chicken broth for the beef bouillon if desired. *Yield: 6 servings.*

Authentic Swedish Meatballs

1/2 cup white bread cubes
1/2 cup hot water
1 pound lean ground beef
1 small red onion, grated
1 teaspoon salt
1 to 1 1/2 teaspoons allspice
1 egg yolk
Butter

Soak the bread cubes in the hot water in a small bowl. Combine the ground beef, onion, salt, allspice, egg yolk and soaked bread in a bowl. Mix with a wooden spoon or clean hands until well blended. Shape into large balls. Heat the butter in a large skillet. Cook the meatballs, 8 to 10 at a time, over medium heat until cooked through.

Turn the meatballs occasionally or shake the skillet slightly to insure the meatballs will retain their shape and brown evenly. Serve hot with mashed potatoes and lingonberry or cranberry preserves. You may shape into very small meatballs and serve with wooden picks for an appetizer.
Yield: 4 to 6 servings.

Company Casserole

2 pounds ground beef
1 tablespoon sugar
1 teaspoon salt
1/8 teaspoon pepper
2 (16-ounce) cans tomato sauce
8 to 12 ounces medium egg noodles
1 cup sour cream
3 ounces cream cheese, softened
2 cups shredded Cheddar cheese

Brown the ground beef in a skillet, stirring until crumbly; drain. Combine the ground beef, sugar, salt, pepper and tomato sauce in a large saucepan. Simmer over medium heat for 20 to 30 minutes.

Cook the egg noodles in boiling water in a saucepan for 4 minutes; drain. Combine the sour cream and cream cheese in a mixing bowl and beat until well blended. Add the cooked egg noodles and mix well.

Layer the egg noodle mixture and ground beef mixture in a greased 9×13-inch baking dish. Bake, covered, at 350 degrees for 30 to 40 minutes. Sprinkle with the Cheddar cheese and bake for 5 minutes longer or until the cheese is melted and bubbly. *Yield: 12 servings.*

Spaghetti with Meat Sauce

1/2 cup finely chopped onion
2 garlic cloves, minced
1/4 cup olive oil
1 pound ground chuck
8 ounces sliced mushrooms
1/4 cup chopped fresh parsley
1 (8-ounce) can tomato sauce
1 (16-ounce) can chopped tomatoes
1 teaspoon salt
1/2 teaspoon pepper
1/4 teaspoon sugar
Pinch of basil
1 cup Burgundy wine
Hot cooked spaghetti

Sauté the onion and garlic in the olive oil in a large skillet or Dutch oven for 5 minutes. Add the ground chuck to the skillet and brown, stirring until crumbly. Add the mushrooms, parsley, tomato sauce, tomatoes, salt, pepper, sugar and basil and mix well.

Simmer, covered, for 1 hour. Add the wine and simmer, covered, for 1 hour longer. Serve over hot cooked spaghetti. This sauce freezes well.
Yield: 6 to 8 servings.

Lasagna

1 pound ground beef
Vegetable oil
Garlic powder to taste
Salt to taste
Pepper to taste
1 teaspoon parsley flakes
Dash of oregano
1 (12-ounce) can tomato paste
1 (14-ounce) can whole tomatoes
2 eggs, beaten
1 cup cottage cheese
1/4 cup grated Parmesan cheese
8 ounces uncooked lasagna noodles
3 cups shredded mozzarella cheese
1/4 cup grated Parmesan cheese

Brown the ground beef in a small amount of oil in a skillet, stirring until crumbly. Add the garlic powder, salt, pepper, parsley flakes and oregano and mix well. Stir in the tomato paste and tomatoes. Simmer for 20 minutes.

Combine the eggs, cottage cheese and 1/4 cup Parmesan cheese in a bowl and mix well. Cook the lasagna noodles in boiling water in a large saucepan for 15 minutes; drain. Skim the excess fat from the top of the ground beef sauce. Pour the skimmed fat into a 9×13-inch baking dish.

Layer the noodles, cheese mixture, ground beef sauce and mozzarella cheese 1/3 at a time in the prepared dish. Sprinkle 1/4 cup Parmesan cheese evenly over the top. Bake, covered, at 350 degrees for 20 minutes. Uncover and bake for 20 minutes longer. Let cool slightly before cutting.
Yield: 8 to 10 servings.

Classic Rack of Lamb

1 (2-pound) rack of lamb
2 tablespoons coarse grain mustard
1/4 cup fine dry bread crumbs
2 tablespoons finely chopped fresh parsley
1/2 teaspoon rosemary
1/8 teaspoon salt
1/8 teaspoon pepper

Trim the outer layer of fat and meat from the top of the rib bones. (Some racks of lamb may be purchased already trimmed.) Trim the remaining fat from the rack. Coat the lamb with the mustard using a pastry brush. Combine the bread crumbs, parsley, rosemary, salt and pepper in a small bowl. Pat the bread crumb mixture evenly over the lamb. Place the lamb, bone side down, on a greased rack in a roasting pan.

Bake at 375 degrees for 1 hour and 15 minutes or until 160 degrees on a meat thermometer. Let stand for 10 minutes before slicing into 8 chops. Garnish with fresh rosemary sprigs. *Yield: 4 servings.*

Marinated Lamb Chops

3/4 cup olive oil
3 teaspoons marjoram
2 teaspoons chopped fresh thyme
2 teaspoons chopped fresh summer savory
1 teaspoon chopped fresh rosemary
1 teaspoon white pepper
4 (1-inch-thick) loin lamb chops

Combine the olive oil, marjoram, thyme, savory, rosemary and pepper in a bowl and mix well. Pour over the lamb chops in a glass dish. Marinate, in the refrigerator, for 24 hours. Grill over hot coals for 4 1/2 to 5 minutes on each side for medium-rare. Serve immediately with mint jelly. *Yield: 4 servings.*

 To substitute dry herbs for fresh, strengths vary in leaves, but the general rule is to use a generous 1/4 teaspoon ground or 1 teaspoon crushed dried leaves for every tablespoon of the finely chopped fresh herb.

Cranberry Pork Roast

1 (1½-pound) boneless pork loin roast
1 (16-ounce) can jellied cranberry sauce
½ cup sugar
½ cup cranberry juice cocktail
1 teaspoon dry mustard
2 tablespoons cornstarch
2 tablespoons cold water
Salt to taste
Hot cooked wild rice

Place the pork roast in a slow cooker. Combine the cranberry sauce, sugar, cranberry juice and dry mustard in a small bowl and mix well. Pour over the pork roast in the slow cooker. Cook on High for 6 to 8 hours.

Remove the pork roast from the slow cooker and keep warm. Skim the fat from the juices in the slow cooker into a saucepan. Add 2 cups of juices from the slow cooker. Bring to a boil over medium-high heat.

Combine the cornstarch and water in a bowl and mix well to make a paste. Stir into the gravy. Season with salt. Cook until thickened, stirring constantly. Serve the pork roast with the prepared gravy and wild rice. *Yield: 4 to 6 servings.*

Honey Grilled Pork Tenderloin

2 (3/4-pound) pork tenderloins
1/3 cup soy sauce
5 garlic cloves, halved
1/2 teaspoon ginger

3 tablespoons honey
2 tablespoons brown sugar
2 teaspoons dark sesame oil

Trim the fat from the tenderloins. Butterfly lengthwise; do not cut all the way through. Place in a shallow, glass dish. Combine the soy sauce, garlic and ginger in a small bowl and mix well. Pour over the tenderloins. Marinate, covered, in the refrigerator for 3 to 10 hours, turning occasionally. Remove the tenderloins and discard the marinade.

Combine the honey, brown sugar and sesame oil in a small saucepan. Cook over low heat until the sugar dissolves, stirring constantly. Place the tenderloins on a greased grill rack. Brush with the honey mixture. Grill over hot coals for 20 minutes, turning and basting frequently. *Yield: 6 to 8 servings.*

Perfect Peachy Pork Tenderloins

2 (1 1/4- to 1 1/2-pound) pork tenderloins
1 (16-ounce) can peach slices in heavy
    syrup
1/2 cup ketchup
1/2 cup packed brown sugar

1/4 cup vinegar
1 tablespoon chili powder
1 tablespoon salt
1 teaspoon garlic powder

Place the tenderloins in a 9×13-inch baking dish. Combine the peaches, ketchup, brown sugar, vinegar, chili powder, salt and garlic powder in a saucepan over medium heat. Bring to a boil. Remove from the heat. Pour over the tenderloins. Bake, covered with foil, at 350 degrees for 30 minutes. Reduce the heat to 325 degrees, uncover and bake for 30 minutes. Slice and serve with the sauce. *Yield: 8 to 10 servings.*

Grilled Pork with Salsa

1/3 cup fresh lime juice
1/4 cup soy sauce
1 teaspoon oregano
1/2 teaspoon thyme
1 (1-pound) pork tenderloin
Salsa

Combine the lime juice, soy sauce, oregano and thyme in a shallow, glass container. Add the tenderloin, turning to coat well. Marinate, covered, in the refrigerator for 4 hours. Remove the tenderloin, reserving the marinade.

Grill the tenderloin over hot coals for 30 minutes or until 160 degrees on a meat thermometer, basting once with the marinade. Slice thinly and serve with salsa and lime wedges. *Yield: 4 servings.*

Zesty Orange Rub for Pork

1/2 cup dried grated orange peel
2 teaspoons onion powder
2 teaspoons sage
1 teaspoon sea salt
1 teaspoon celery salt
1/2 teaspoon freshly ground pepper
2 to 4 teaspoons olive oil

Combine the orange peel, onion powder, sage, sea salt, celery salt, pepper and olive oil in a small bowl and mix well. Rub onto pork roasts, pork tenderloins or pork chops before roasting or grilling. You may also mix in 1/2 cup bread crumbs for a crumb crust. *Yield: Variable.*

West African Red Beans and R

1 pound dried red kidney beans
2 quarts water
2 to 3 tablespoons vegetable oil or
   bacon drippings
1 large onion, chopped
1 green bell pepper, chopped
4 ribs celery, chopped
4 garlic cloves, minced
1 (14-ounce) can chopped tomatoes

5 cups cold water
3/4 to 1 teaspoon dried red pe...
1 bay leaf
1 teaspoon thyme
1 smoked ham hock or meaty ham
   bone
1 pound smoked sausage link, sliced,
   browned
5 cups cooked white rice

Sort and rinse the beans. Place in a large saucepan. Add 2 quarts water and let soak for 8 to 10 hours or bring to a boil, remove from the heat, and let stand, covered, for 1 hour. Drain, rinse and drain again.

Heat the oil in a large stockpot. Sauté the onion, bell pepper, celery and garlic in the oil for 6 minutes. Add the tomatoes and 5 cups water. Add the beans, red pepper flakes, bay leaf, thyme and ham hock.

Bring to a boil and reduce the heat. Simmer, covered, for 1 1/2 to 2 hours or until the beans are tender, stirring frequently. Add the sausage during the last 30 minutes of cooking time. Remove the bay leaf before serving. Serve over the rice with jalapeño corn bread. *Yield: 8 to 10 servings.*

Sesame Baked Chicken

1 egg, lightly beaten
1/2 cup milk
1 cup flour
1/4 cup chopped pecans
2 teaspoons salt
2 teaspoons sesame seeds
1 teaspoon baking powder
1/4 teaspoon pepper
1/2 cup (1 stick) butter
1 (3-pound) roasting chicken, cut up

Combine the egg and milk in a small bowl. Combine the flour, pecans, salt, sesame seeds, baking powder and pepper in a separate bowl. Melt the butter in a 9×13-inch baking dish in a 400-degree oven. Dip the chicken into the egg mixture and then dip into the flour mixture.

Place the chicken in the melted butter in the baking dish, turning the chicken to coat well. Bake at 400 degrees for 50 minutes, turning the chicken after 30 minutes. Yield: 4 servings.

Sweet and Sticky Grilled Chicken

2 pounds chicken pieces
1/4 cup poultry seasoning
1/4 cup honey
2 tablespoons fresh lemon juice
2 tablespoons poultry seasoning

Rinse the chicken and pat dry. Sprinkle the chicken with 1/4 cup poultry seasoning. Place in a greased 9×13-inch glass baking dish. Bake at 350 degrees for 40 minutes.

Combine the honey, lemon juice, and 2 tablespoons poultry seasoning in a small bowl and mix well. Baste the chicken with the honey mixture. Grill over hot coals for 10 minutes, turning and basting frequently. *Yield: 4 servings.*

Crispy Chicken Breast

1/2 cup mayonnaise
3 tablespoons prepared mustard
1/2 cup (1 stick) butter or margarine, melted
8 boneless skinless chicken breasts
1 (8-ounce) package herb-seasoned stuffing mix, crushed

Combine the mayonnaise, mustard and melted butter in a bowl and mix well. Dip the chicken in the mayonnaise mixture and then dip in the crushed stuffing mix, turning to coat well. Place the prepared chicken in a greased 9×9-inch baking dish. Mix the remaining stuffing mix with the remaining mayonnaise mixture and sprinkle around the chicken in the baking dish. Bake, covered, at 350 degrees for 1 hour. Bake, uncovered, for 30 minutes longer. *Yield: 6 to 8 servings.*

Chicken with Fruited Wild Rice

1 tablespoon flour
1 large oven cooking bag
1 (6-ounce) package long-grain wild rice
1 (3-ounce) package craisins
1 (2-ounce) package slivered almonds, toasted
1 (10-ounce) can chicken broth
1 1/3 cups water
4 boneless skinless chicken breasts

Add the flour to the cooking bag and shake to coat well. Remove the seasoning packet from the rice and reserve 1 teaspoon of the seasoning mix. Combine the remaining seasoning mix, rice, craisins, almonds, chicken broth and water in a bowl and mix well. Pour into the prepared oven bag.

Rub the chicken with the reserved seasoning mix. Place in the oven bag. Secure the bag with the tie and place in a 9×13-inch baking dish. Cut 6 small slits in the oven bag.

Bake at 350 degrees for 45 minutes. You may substitute 4 Cornish game hens for the chicken breasts. *Yield: 4 servings.*

Hot Chicken Salad

2 cups chopped cooked chicken
2 cups thinly sliced celery
1 cup croutons
1/2 cup mayonnaise
1/2 cup cream of chicken soup
1/2 cup slivered almonds, toasted

2 tablespoons lemon juice
2 teaspoons dried minced onion
1/2 teaspoon salt
1 cup croutons
1/2 cup shredded Cheddar cheese

Combine the chicken, celery, 1 cup croutons, mayonnaise, cream of chicken soup, almonds, lemon juice, minced onion and salt in a large bowl. Spoon into a small baking dish. Sprinkle with 1 cup croutons and the Cheddar cheese. Bake at 450 degrees for 15 minutes or until bubbly. *Yield: 4 servings.*

Chicken Bundles

8 ounces cream cheese, softened
1/4 to 1/2 cup chopped onion
1/4 cup milk
2 (8-count) cans refrigerator
   crescent rolls

4 boneless skinless chicken breasts,
   cooked, chopped
Freshly grated Parmesan cheese

Combine the cream cheese, onion and milk in a small bowl and mix well. Roll out the crescent roll dough, separate into 8 rectangles and press to seal the perforations. Add the chicken to the cream cheese mixture and mix well. Spoon the chicken mixture into the center of each dough rectangle. Roll up and pinch each end to seal. Roll in Parmesan cheese and place in a glass baking dish. Bake at 350 degrees for 30 minutes or until golden brown. *Yield: 8 servings.*

 *The Chicken Bundles are good served with **French Onion Rice.** Combine 1 cup uncooked white rice, 1 (10-ounce) can French onion soup, and 1 soup can water in a saucepan. Cook, covered, for 30 minutes or until the water is absorbed.*

Company Chicken Casserole

$1/2$ cup (1 stick) butter
$1/2$ cup chopped onion
$1/2$ cup chopped green bell pepper
2 (10-ounce) cans cream of mushroom soup
3 cups chopped cooked chicken
2 cups shredded sharp Cheddar cheese
1 (4-ounce) can mushrooms
1 (2-ounce) package slivered almonds
$1/4$ cup chopped pimentos
1 (6-ounce) package long-grain wild rice

Melt the butter in a skillet. Sauté the onion and bell pepper in the skillet until tender. Combine the soup, chicken, cheese, mushrooms, almonds and pimentos in a large bowl and mix well.

Prepare the wild rice according to the package directions. Stir into the chicken mixture. Add the prepared onion and bell pepper. Spoon into a 9×12-inch baking dish. Bake at 325 degrees for 20 to 30 minutes or until bubbly. *Yield: 12 to 15 servings.*

Chicken Potpie

1 *cup chopped onion*
1 *cup chopped celery*
1 *cup sliced carrot*
1/3 *cup butter, melted*
1/2 *cup flour*
2 *cups chicken broth*
1 *cup milk or half-and-half*
1 *teaspoon salt*
1/4 *teaspoon pepper*
4 *cups chopped cooked chicken*
1 *(1-crust) refrigerator pie pastry*

Sauté the onion, celery and carrot in the melted butter in a skillet for 10 minutes. Add the flour and cook for 1 minute, stirring constantly. Combine the chicken broth and milk in a small bowl and mix well. Stir into the onion mixture. Cook over medium heat until thickened and bubbly, stirring constantly. Add the salt and pepper. Stir in the chicken.

Pour into a 9×13-inch baking dish. Roll out the pastry to fit the baking dish. Place on top of the mixture, securing around the edge. Cut slits in the pastry. Bake at 400 degrees for 40 minutes. You may also add other vegetables, such as green peas, if desired. *Yield: 6 to 8 servings.*

Spicy African Chicken Stew

1 tablespoon vegetable oil
1 pound boneless skinless chicken breasts, cut into 1-inch pieces
1 1/2 cups chopped onion
2 garlic cloves, minced
1 (28-ounce) can stewed tomatoes
1/4 cup creamy peanut butter
1/2 teaspoon chili powder
1/2 teaspoon salt
1/4 teaspoon crushed red pepper flakes
3 cups hot cooked rice or pasta
1/2 cup chopped dry roasted peanuts

Heat the oil in a large skillet over medium-high heat. Add the chicken, onion and garlic. Cook for 5 minutes or until the chicken is brown and onion is tender. Stir in the tomatoes, peanut butter, chili powder, salt and red pepper flakes.

Bring to a boil. Reduce the heat and simmer, covered, for 35 minutes. Serve over the rice or pasta. Sprinkle with the peanuts. *Yield: 6 servings*.

Linguine with Chicken, Sun-Dried Tomatoes and Gorgonzola

1/2 cup drained, chopped oil-pack sun-dried tomatoes,
reserve 2 tablespoons oil
2 boneless skinless chicken breasts, cut into strips
4 garlic cloves, minced
1/2 cup chopped fresh basil
1 cup chicken broth
1/2 cup crumbled Gorgonzola cheese
1/4 cup prosciutto, sliced
1/2 teaspoon hot red pepper flakes
Salt to taste
Pepper to taste
16 ounces linguine, cooked

Heat the reserved oil from the sun-dried tomatoes in a large skillet. Add the chicken and sauté until cooked through. Remove to a bowl. Add the garlic to the skillet and sauté for 1 minute.

Add the sun-dried tomatoes, cooked chicken, basil, broth, Gorgonzola cheese and prosciutto to the skillet. Bring to a boil. Add the red pepper flakes, salt and pepper. Add the hot cooked linguine and toss to mix well.
Yield: 4 servings.

Marinated Wild Duck Breasts

1 cup merlot
1 cup balsamic or red wine vinegar
1 cup Allegro game tame marinade
1/4 cup olive oil
2 tablespoons chopped garlic
1 tablespoon oregano
1 tablespoon crushed dried basil
6 to 8 boneless wild duck breast halves

Combine the merlot, balsamic vinegar, game tame marinade, olive oil, garlic, oregano and basil in a large sealable plastic bag. Add the duck. Marinate, in the refrigerator, for 24 to 48 hours, turning several times.

Grill the duck over hot coals for 2 minutes per side or until 180 degrees on a meat thermometer, basting during grilling; do not overcook. Slice across the grain to serve. Serve hot or cold.
Yield: 4 servings as an entrée or 6 to 8 servings as an appetizer.

Baked Fish Fillets

2 ribs celery, chopped
1 small onion, chopped
1/4 cup water
3 tablespoons butter
1/4 cup flour
1 cup milk
Salt to taste
Pepper to taste
1 bay leaf
1 teaspoon Tabasco sauce
3 tablespoons dry sherry
1 to 1 1/2 pounds fish fillets

Sauté the celery and onion in the water in a skillet until tender. Set aside. Melt the butter in a saucepan. Add the flour and cook until bubbly, stirring constantly. Add the milk gradually and cook until thickened to make a cream sauce. Add the salt, pepper, bay leaf, Tabasco sauce and sherry. Stir in the prepared celery and onion.

Spoon some of the sauce mixture onto aluminum foil squares. Place 2 or 3 fish fillets on top and fold up to make a packet. (The size of the fish will determine how many packets you will have.)

Place the packets on a baking sheet or in a baking dish. Bake at 350 degrees for 25 to 30 minutes. You may also grill the packets over hot coals. Unwrap the packets and transfer the fish to a platter before serving. Spoon the sauce over the fish. *Yield: 4 to 6 servings.*

Salmon, Leek and Potato Gratin

1³/₄ *pounds potatoes, peeled, cooked, mashed*
³/₄ *cup (1¹/₂ sticks) unsalted butter, softened*
3 small leeks, thinly sliced
5 ounces salmon fillet, skinned
6 ounces smoked salmon, chopped
1¹/₄ *cups heavy cream*
Salt to taste
Pepper to taste
³/₄ *cup shredded Swiss cheese*
3 tablespoons unsalted butter, cut into pieces

Combine the mashed potatoes and half of the ³/₄ cup butter in a bowl and mix well; keep warm. Melt the remaining half of the ³/₄ cup butter in a skillet over low heat. Add the leeks and sauté for 2 to 3 minutes. Spread the leeks over the bottom of an oval gratin dish; set aside.

Steam the salmon fillet in a steamer basket for 5 to 10 minutes or until the fish flakes easily with a fork. Flake the fish into bite-size pieces and add to the mashed potatoes. Add the smoked salmon and mix gently.

Bring the cream to a boil in a saucepan. Add the mashed potato and salmon mixture. Season with salt and pepper. Spoon over the leeks in the gratin dish. Sprinkle with the Swiss cheese. Dot with 3 tablespoons butter. Brown under the broiler for 2 to 3 minutes or until light brown. Garnish with fresh dill sprigs. *Yield: 6 servings.*

Marinated Salmon

3 to 4 green onions, chopped
1/2 cup (1 stick) butter
1/4 cup soy sauce
1 tablespoon (or more) minced
  fresh garlic
1 or 2 large salmon fillets

Sauté the green onions in the butter in a skillet until tender. Add the soy sauce and garlic and mix well. Place the salmon fillets in a glass baking dish. Score the salmon several times. Pour the prepared marinade over the salmon. Marinate, covered, in the refrigerator for 1 hour. Remove from the marinade. Bake or grill until cooked through and the fish flakes easily. Yield: 2 to 4 servings.

Grilled Swordfish with Caper Sauce

1/2 cup dry white wine
5 garlic cloves, minced
1 teaspoon chopped fresh rosemary
4 (4-ounce) swordfish steaks
1/4 teaspoon salt
1/4 teaspoon pepper
1 teaspoon chopped fresh rosemary
1/3 cup lemon juice
3 tablespoons basil olive oil
1 tablespoon capers, drained
3 tablespoons fine dry bread crumbs

Combine the wine, garlic and 1 teaspoon rosemary in an 8-inch square glass baking dish. Sprinkle the swordfish with salt and pepper. Place the swordfish in the baking dish, turning to coat with the wine mixture. Marinate, covered, in the refrigerator for 1 hour or more. Remove the fish to a greased grill rack; discarding the marinade.

Grill over hot coals, with the grill lid closed, for 4 to 5 minutes on each side. Combine 1 teaspoon rosemary, lemon juice, olive oil, capers and bread crumbs in a small bowl; mix well. Spoon over the warm fish and serve immediately. Yield: 4 servings.

Tuna with Mango Salsa

Tuna

[...] r
[...]ced fresh gingerroot
[...] mango
[...] hopped candied ginger
[...] chopped red bell pepper
[...] chopped green onions
2 tablesp[...] chopped fresh cilantro
Juice of 1 lime
4 dashes Tabasco sauce

4 tuna steaks
Olive oil
Salt to taste
Pepper to taste

For the salsa, heat the mango nectar and fresh gingerroot in a saucepan over medium heat. Cook for 15 minutes or until thickened and reduced by half, stirring occasionally. Remove from the heat and cool slightly. Add the mango, candied ginger, bell pepper, green onions, cilantro, lime juice and Tabasco sauce; mix well. Chill, covered, for several hours.

For the tuna, brush the tuna steaks with olive oil. Sprinkle with salt and pepper. Grill over hot coals for 10 to 15 minutes for rare and 20 to 25 minutes for well done. Serve the tuna warm with a generous spoonful of the mango salsa. *Yield: 4 servings*.

Gulf Shrimp Newspaper

4 ribs celery with leaves, chopped
1 to 2 green bell peppers, coarsely
  chopped
2 lemons or limes, halved
Salt to taste
3 tablespoons Old Bay seasoning
Tabasco sauce to taste
16 red potatoes
12 small onions, peeled

12 chicken thighs
2 pounds kielbasa, c
12 ears corn, halved
3 tablespoons Old Bay
2 2/3 pounds unpeeled fr
3 clean brown grocery ba
1/2 cup (1 stick) butter, me
Cocktail sauce
4 lemons or limes, cut into wedges

Fill a large stockpot with water. Add the celery, bell peppers, lemon halves, salt, 3 tablespoons Old Bay seasoning, Tabasco sauce, potatoes, onions, chicken and kielbasa. Bring to a boil and cook for 20 minutes. Add the corn and 3 tablespoons Old Bay seasoning. Cook for 6 minutes. Add the shrimp and cook for 2 to 3 minutes or until pink; drain.

Spoon the shrimp mixture into the grocery bags. Cover a table with newspapers. Place the bags on the tables, split the bags down the middle and serve from the bags. Serve with the melted butter, cocktail sauce and lemon wedges. No utensils are needed. Let guests peel their shrimp and pick up the food with their hands. *Yield: 8 servings.*

Low Georgia Boil

1 can Tony Chachere's crab boil mix
20 small red potatoes
10 large carrots, halved
20 small ears of corn
20 small peeled onions

3 packages Polish sausage, cut into
   chunks
20 small yellow squash
2 to 3 pounds unpeeled fresh shrimp

Fill a 20-quart stockpot half full with water. Bring to a boil and add the crab boil mix. Add the potatoes and carrots and boil for 15 minutes. Add the corn and onions and boil for 15 minutes longer. Add the sausage and squash and boil for 15 minutes longer.

Boil for another 15 minutes. Add the shrimp and turn off the heat. Let stand, covered, for 10 minutes. Drain and spoon into large containers to serve. Serve with hot crusty bread. *Yield: 10 to 12 servings.*

Shrimp Delight

1 onion, sliced
2 garlic cloves, minced
1 tablespoon butter
1 (10-ounce) can cream of mushroom
   soup

1/4 cup chili sauce
2 cups peeled cooked shrimp
1 cup sour cream
Hot cooked rice

Sauté the onion and garlic in the butter in a skillet until tender. Add the soup, chili sauce and shrimp. Cook until thickened. Stir in the sour cream and cook until heated through. Spoon over hot cooked rice. Serve with a green salad and hot crusty bread. *Yield: 4 or 5 servings.*

Shrimp, Tomato and Herb Pasta

1/4 cup olive oil
4 garlic cloves, minced
1/2 teaspoon hot red pepper flakes
1 teaspoon oregano
1 teaspoon basil
1 pound uncooked peeled shrimp
3/4 pound cherry tomatoes
Salt to taste

Freshly ground pepper to taste
8 ounces hot cooked pasta
1/4 cup grated Parmesan cheese
1/4 cup chopped fresh parsley
1/4 cup chopped fresh basil
Grated zest of 1 lemon

Heat the olive oil in a large skillet over medium heat. Sauté the garlic, red pepper flakes. oregano, 1 teaspoon basil and shrimp for 2 minutes or until the shrimp turn pink. Add the tomatoes, salt and pepper and cook for 2 to 3 minutes or until the tomatoes are tender.

Add the cooked pasta and toss until well mixed. Spoon into a large pasta bowl. Sprinkle with the Parmesan cheese, parsley, 1/4 cup basil and lemon zest and toss gently. Serve with additional grated Parmesan cheese.
Yield: 2 to 4 servings.

aside Pasta

es sun-dried tomatoes, chopped
1 cup boiling water
1/2 cup olive oil
1 pound deveined peeled shrimp
resh asparagus, snapped into 11/2-inch pieces
1 bunch green onions, chopped
1/4 cup pine nuts
1/2 cup sliced black olives
Chopped fresh basil to taste
8 ounces linguine, cooked, drained
1/4 cup freshly grated Parmesan cheese
Salt to taste
Pepper to taste
1/4 cup freshly grated Parmesan cheese
1 bunch green onions, chopped

Soak the sun-dried tomatoes in the boiling water in a small bowl for
3 to 5 minutes; drain. Heat the olive oil in a 10-inch skillet over medium
heat. Sauté the shrimp in the oil for 2 minutes. Add the asparagus, 1 bunch
green onions, pine nuts, black olives and basil. Cook for 2 minutes, stirring
frequently.

Combine the cooked linguine, shrimp mixture and 1/4 cup Parmesan cheese
in a large pasta bowl and toss to mix well. Season with the salt and pepper.
Top with 1/4 cup Parmesan cheese and 1 bunch green onions. Serve with a
tossed green salad and hot crusty bread. Yield: 4 servings.

Linguine with White Clam Sauce

1 onion, chopped
1/2 cup (1 stick) butter
8 ounces fresh mushrooms, capped, sliced
3 tablespoons flour
1 1/2 cups milk
1/4 cup chopped fresh parsley
1/4 cup chopped green onions

4 (7-ounce) cans minced clams, drained, reserving juice
3 tablespoons grated Parmesan cheese
Salt to taste
White pepper to taste
Garlic powder to taste
Hot cooked linguine

Sauté the onion in the butter in a skillet until tender. Add the mushrooms and flour and stir to form a paste. Add the milk and cook until thickened, stirring constantly. Add the parsley, green onions and reserved juice from the clams. Add the Parmesan cheese, salt, white pepper and garlic powder and mix well. Cook until the green onions are tender. Stir in the clams and simmer for 5 minutes. Serve over the hot cooked linguine. Garnish with fresh parsley. Spinach linguine makes an especially attractive presentation. Serve with a green salad and French bread. *Yield: 6 servings.*

Tomato and Feta Spaghetti Alfredo

2 red bell peppers
3 elephant garlic cloves
Olive oil
1/2 pound (2 sticks) butter
1 cup heavy cream
1/4 cup grated Parmesan cheese

16 ounces cooked spaghetti
8 ounces assorted wild mushrooms
1 cup fresh basil, torn into pieces
1/2 cup kalamata olives, sliced
1/2 cup feta cheese, crumbled
2 cups chopped fresh tomatoes

Roast the bell peppers in a 350-degree oven for 30 minutes. Let cool, remove the skins and cut into strips. Place the garlic in foil; drizzle with a small amount of olive oil. Wrap the garlic loosely in the foil. Roast the garlic in a 350-degree oven for 30 minutes. Remove from the foil and chop into small pieces. Combine the butter, cream and Parmesan cheese in a saucepan. Cook over medium heat until thickened and the butter is melted, stirring frequently. Combine the prepared roasted bell peppers, garlic, cooked pasta and prepared Alfredo sauce in a large pasta bowl and toss to mix well. Top with the mushrooms, basil, olives, feta cheese and tomatoes. Serve immediately. *Yield: 4 servings.*

Spinach Cannelloni

2 tablespoons butter
2 (10-ounce) packages frozen spinach, thawed, drained
15 ounces ricotta cheese
1/4 cup freshly grated Parmesan cheese
1/4 cup freshly grated Romano cheese
1 cup shredded mozzarella cheese
1/4 teaspoon nutmeg
2 eggs, beaten
1 jar chunky garden-style pasta sauce
1 (1-pound) package egg roll skins
1 cup shredded mozzarella cheese

Melt the butter in a skillet over medium-high heat. Add the spinach and cook for 3 minutes. Stir in the ricotta cheese and cook for 3 minutes. Add the Parmesan cheese, Romano cheese, 1 cup mozzarella cheese, nutmeg and eggs. Mix well and remove from the heat.

Pour a small amount of the pasta sauce into the bottom of a 10×15-inch baking dish. Place 1 egg roll skin on a flat surface. Spoon 1/4 cup of the spinach mixture on the egg roll skin. Roll up and seal the edge using a small amount of water if necessary. Repeat using all of the spinach mixture.

Place the cannelloni seam side down in the prepared baking dish. Cover with the remaining pasta sauce. Bake, covered with foil, at 350 degrees for 45 minutes. Remove the foil and sprinkle with 1 cup mozzarella cheese. Bake for 5 minutes longer or until the cheese is melted. Yield: 6 to 8 servings.

Breads

Elizabeth Beach Kiser

Elizabeth Beach Kiser, a native of Clarksville, Tennessee, does most of her work as a commission artist from her home on Old Hickory Lake in the Nashville, Tennessee, area. Elizabeth, a wife and mother of three, specializes in portraits and human figures. She works in oil and pastels. A graduate of the Mississippi University for Women with a BFA and major in commercial art, she began her art career in Nashville at the United Methodist Publishing House. She also worked for Aladdin Industries creating original art for lunchboxes. Elizabeth describes her subject matter as endless as her love and enjoyment for her craft.

Shown on overleaf: *Delighted*

Cranberry Oatmeal Nut Bread

2 cups boiling water
1 1/2 cups rolled oats
1 1/2 cups dried cranberries
2 tablespoons dry yeast
1/2 cup warm water
1/2 cup packed brown sugar
2 teaspoons salt
1/4 cup vegetable oil
2 cups flour
1 cup chopped walnuts
2 1/2 cups flour
1 egg, beaten with 1 tablespoon cold water
Rolled oats for sprinkling

Pour the boiling water over the oats and dried cranberries in a medium bowl. Stir and cover. Let stand for 45 minutes. Dissolve the yeast into the warm water (105 to 115 degrees) in a large mixing bowl. Add the brown sugar, salt, oil, 2 cups flour, walnuts and the oat and cranberry mixture. Beat with a dough whisk or heavy spoon for 2 minutes. Add 2 1/2 cups flour 1/4 cup at a time, mixing well until the dough begins to pull away from the side of the bowl.

Place the dough in a greased bowl, turning to coat the dough. Let rise, covered, for 1 hour or until doubled in size. Turn the dough out onto a lightly floured surface and divide in half. Shape into 2 loaves. Place the loaves into 2 greased loaf pans. Let rise, covered, for 45 minutes. Brush each loaf with the egg wash. Sprinkle with dry oats if desired. Bake at 375 degrees for 30 to 35 minutes or until browned. Remove from the pans immediately and let cool on a wire rack. Yield: 2 loaves.

Dilly Bread

1 envelope dry yeast
1/4 cup warm water
1 cup cottage cheese
2 tablespoons sugar
1 egg, beaten
1 tablespoon butter, softened
1 tablespoon finely chopped onion
1/2 teaspoon onion powder
2 teaspoons dillseeds
1 teaspoon salt
1/4 teaspoon baking soda
2 1/4 to 2 1/2 cups flour

Dissolve the yeast in the warm water in a bowl; set aside. Combine the cottage cheese, sugar, egg, butter, onion and yeast mixture in a large bowl. Combine the onion powder, dillseeds, salt, baking soda and flour in a separate bowl. Add the flour mixture to the cottage cheese mixture gradually, stirring to form a stiff dough. Let rise, covered, in a warm place for 50 to 60 minutes or until doubled in size.

Punch the dough down and place in a greased ovenproof 8-inch bowl, turning to coat the dough. Let rise in a warm place for 30 to 40 minutes or until doubled in size. Bake at 350 degrees for 30 to 40 minutes.

Brush the top of the bread with melted butter and sprinkle with coarse salt if desired. This is a hearty bread that is delicious served with soups.
Yield: 10 to 12 servings.

Feta Cheese Bread

2 cups flour
2 teaspoons sugar
$^1/_2$ teaspoon salt
1 envelope quick-rise yeast
1 $^1/_2$ cups milk
$^1/_4$ cup water
$^1/_4$ cup shortening
2 cups flour
$^1/_4$ cup ($^1/_2$ stick) butter, softened, divided
4 ounces crumbled feta cheese
2 tablespoons butter, melted

Combine 2 cups flour, sugar, salt and yeast in a large mixing bowl. Combine the milk, water and shortening in a small saucepan. Cook over medium heat until the shortening melts. Let cool to 125 to 130 degrees. Add the milk mixture to the flour mixture gradually, beating well. Stir in 2 cups flour gradually until a soft dough forms. Turn the dough out onto a well-floured surface. Knead 4 or 5 times. Divide the dough in half.

Roll each half into an 8×16-inch rectangle. Spread 2 tablespoons butter over each rectangle. Sprinkle each rectangle with feta cheese. Roll the dough up, as for a jelly roll, starting at the long side; pinch the seam to seal. Fold the ends under and place seam side down in 2 greased French bread pans. Brush both loaves with the 2 tablespoons melted butter.

Let rise, covered, in a warm place for 45 to 60 minutes. Bake at 375 degrees for 15 minutes. Reduce the heat to 350 degrees and bake for 20 minutes or until the loaves sound hollow when tapped. Remove from the pans immediately. *Yield: 2 loaves.*

Bread Machine Banana Granola Bread

2/3 cup water
1 1/4 cups white bread flour
3/4 cup wheat bread flour
4 teaspoons nonfat dry milk powder
1 teaspoon salt
4 teaspoons butter, softened
1/2 cup mashed bananas
1/2 cup granola
1/4 cup chopped walnuts
1/4 cup banana chips
1 1/2 teaspoons dry yeast
1 teaspoon quick-rise yeast

Add the water, white bread flour, wheat bread flour, dry milk powder, salt, butter, mashed bananas, granola, walnuts, banana chips, dry yeast and quick-rise yeast to the bread machine pan in the order listed in the owner's manual.

Set the machine on the basic bread-making setting following the manufacturer's directions. Set the machine on the normal to medium color setting. Remove the loaf to a wire rack to cool when the baking cycle is complete. Yield: 1 regular loaf.

Bread Machine Honey Wheat Bread

3/4 cup water
1 1/2 cups white bread flour
1/2 cup wheat bread flour
1 tablespoon nonfat dry milk powder
1 tablespoon honey
1 teaspoon salt
1 tablespoon butter
1 teaspoon quick-rise yeast

Combine the water, white bread flour, wheat bread flour, dry milk powder, honey, salt, butter and yeast in a bread machine pan in the order listed in the owner's manual.

Set the machine on the basic bread-making setting following the manufacturer's directions. Set the machine on the normal to medium color setting. Remove the loaf to a wire rack to cool when the baking cycle is complete. Yield: 1 regular loaf.

Light Whole Wheat Bread

5 teaspoons dry yeast
1 teaspoon sugar
1/2 cup (95 to 105 degrees) warm
    water
3 cups hot (150 degrees) water
1/4 cup (1/2 stick) butter
1/3 cup sugar, less 1 teaspoon

2 tablespoons salt
2 cups whole wheat bread flour
3 cups white bread flour
3 tablespoons vital wheat gluten
1 egg, lightly beaten
3 to 3 1/2 cups white bread flour

Dissolve the yeast and 1 teaspoon sugar in the warm water in a bowl. Let stand for 5 to 10 minutes. Pour 3 cups hot water over the butter, sugar and salt in a large mixing bowl. Stir until the butter is melted and let cool slightly. Stir in the whole wheat bread flour, 3 cups white bread flour and wheat gluten and mix well. Add the yeast mixture and mix well. Beat in the egg. Beat for 3 minutes. Let stand, covered, for 10 minutes or until the dough becomes spongy. Add 3 to 3 1/2 cups white bread flour 1/2 cup at a time, mixing until the dough pulls away from the side of the bowl.

Turn the dough out onto a floured surface and knead in any remaining flour until the dough is no longer sticky. Knead for 10 minutes or until the dough is smooth and elastic. Place the dough in a greased bowl, turning to coat the dough. Let rise, covered, for 45 minutes or until doubled in size. Punch the dough down and turn out onto a floured surface. Knead the dough for 2 to 3 minutes.

Divide the dough into 3 equal parts. Place into greased loaf pans. Let stand, covered, for 10 minutes. Turn the dough out onto a floured surface and roll into a 9×11-inch rectangle. Roll up as for a jelly roll, starting with the short end. Pinch the seam to seal. Return to the loaf pan. Repeat for all loaves. Let rise, covered, for 45 minutes or until doubled in size.

Bake at 400 degrees for 10 minutes. Reduce the heat to 350 degrees. Bake for 30 to 35 minutes or until loaves sound hollow when tapped. Remove from the pans immediately and let cool on wire racks. Brush with melted butter. *Yield: 3 loaves.*

Refrigerator Rolls

1 *cup boiling water*
1 *cup shortening*
1 *cup sugar*
1 1/2 *teaspoons salt*

2 *eggs, beaten*
2 *envelopes dry yeast*
1 *cup warm water*
6 *cups unbleached flour*

Combine the boiling water, shortening, sugar and salt in a bowl and stir until the shortening melts and the sugar is dissolved. Let cool and add the eggs. Dissolve the yeast in the warm water in a mixing bowl. Add the yeast to the shortening mixture. Add the flour and mix well. Let rise, covered, for 3 hours or until doubled in size. These may also rise overnight in the refrigerator. Punch down the dough and roll out on a floured surface. Cut out rolls with a biscuit cutter. Place on a greased baking sheet and fold the dough over. Let rise, covered loosely, for 3 hours or until doubled in size. Bake at 400 degrees for 12 to 15 minutes or until light brown. *Yield: 100 rolls.*

Whole Wheat Rolls

1 *envelope dry yeast*
1/4 *cup sugar*
1 3/4 *cups warm water*
2 *cups whole wheat flour*

1 3/4 *cups all-purpose flour*
1 1/2 *teaspoons salt*
3/4 *cup shortening*

Dissolve the yeast and sugar in the warm water in a large bowl. Stir until the sugar is dissolved. Add the whole wheat flour, all-purpose flour, salt and shortening and mix well. (More flour may be added if dough is too soft.) Let rise for 30 minutes. Punch the dough down. Spoon into greased muffin tins. Let rise for 1 hour or until doubled in size. Bake at 375 degrees for 10 minutes. *Yield: 1 dozen.*

Try adding a small handful of oat bran or bran flakes to the Whole Wheat Rolls or your other favorite roll recipe for added texture.

Almond Poppy Seed Bread

3 cups flour, sifted
2¼ cups sugar
1½ teaspoons baking soda
1½ teaspoons salt ·
1½ teaspoons butter flavoring
1½ teaspoons almond extract
1½ teaspoons vanilla extract
1½ cups milk

1½ tablespoons poppy seeds
1 cup plus 2 tablespoons vegetable oil
3 eggs
¼ cup orange juice
¾ cup sugar
¼ teaspoon butter flavoring
¼ teaspoon almond extract
¼ teaspoon vanilla extract

Combine the flour, 2¼ cups sugar, baking soda, salt, 1½ teaspoons butter flavoring, 1½ teaspoons almond extract, 1½ teaspoons vanilla extract, milk, poppy seeds, oil and eggs in a large bowl and mix for 2 minutes with a spoon. Pour into 2 large loaf pans or 3 small loaf pans. Bake at 325 degrees for 1 hour to 1 hour and 20 minutes.

Combine the orange juice, ¾ cup sugar, ¼ teaspoon butter flavoring, ¼ teaspoon almond extract and ¼ teaspoon vanilla extract in a small saucepan and mix well. Bring to a boil and boil for 1 minute. Pour over the hot loaves. Let stand for 20 minutes before slicing. *Yield: 2 loaves.*

Dried Apricot Pecan Bread

1 cup boiling water
1 1/2 cups dried apricot halves, coarsely chopped
3 tablespoons unsalted butter
1 cup sugar
2 cups unbleached flour
1 1/2 teaspoons baking soda
1/2 teaspoon salt
1/2 cup whole wheat flour
1 cup chopped pecans
2 eggs, beaten
1/2 cup orange juice

Pour the boiling water over the dried apricots, butter and sugar in a large mixing bowl. Mix well and let cool. Stir the unbleached flour, baking soda and salt into the apricot mixture. Add the whole wheat flour, pecans, eggs and orange juice. Beat until well mixed; do not overmix. Pour into 2 greased and floured 3 1/2x7 1/4-inch loaf pans.

Let stand for 15 minutes before baking. Bake at 350 degrees for 55 to 60 minutes or until a wooden pick inserted in the center comes out clean. Remove from the pans and let cool on wire racks. Wrap in plastic wrap and chill for 8 to 10 hours before serving. *Yield: 2 loaves.*

Make elegant sandwiches for a party or holiday gathering. Sandwich very thinly sliced smoked turkey or black forest ham between slices of the Dried Apricot Pecan Bread. This bread is also delicious toasted and served plain or with butter or cream cheese.

Banana Bread

1/2 cup shortening, melted
1/2 cup (1 stick) butter or margarine, melted
3 cups sugar
4 eggs, beaten
1/2 cup buttermilk
6 bananas, mashed
3 1/2 cups flour
2 teaspoons baking soda
1/2 teaspoon salt
2 teaspoons vanilla extract
1 cup chopped pecans (optional)

Combine the melted shortening and butter in a large bowl. Stir in the sugar. Add the eggs, buttermilk and bananas and mix well. Combine the flour, baking soda and salt in a separate bowl. Add to the banana mixture and mix well. Stir in the vanilla and pecans.

Pour into 2 large greased loaf pans or 4 smaller loaf pans. Bake at 350 degrees for 35 to 40 minutes or until a wooden pick inserted in the center comes out clean. *Yield: 2 loaves.*

 Try combining 8 ounces cream cheese and 2 teaspoons orange juice concentrate in a small bowl and mix well. Spread on toasted slices of Banana Bread.

Chocolate Chip Banana Bread

3 bananas
1 cup sugar
1 egg, beaten
$1/4$ cup ($1/2$ stick) butter, melted and cooled
$1 1/2$ cups sifted flour
1 teaspoon salt
1 teaspoon baking soda
1 cup (6 ounces) chocolate chips

Mash the bananas in a large bowl. Add the sugar, egg, melted butter, flour, salt and baking soda and mix well. Stir in the chocolate chips. Pour into a greased loaf pan.

Bake at 325 degrees for 1 hour or until a wooden pick inserted in the center comes out clean. Let cool in the pan on a wire rack for 15 minutes. Remove from the pan. This bread freezes well. *Yield: 1 loaf.*

Lemon Poppy Seed Bread

3 tablespoons poppy seeds
1/2 cup milk
5 tablespoons unsalted butter, softened
1 cup sugar
2 eggs
1 1/2 cups unbleached flour
1 teaspoon baking powder
Grated zest of 2 lemons
1/4 teaspoon salt

Combine the poppy seeds and milk in a small bowl. Let stand for 1 hour. Cream the butter and sugar in a large mixing bowl until light and fluffy. Add the eggs 1 at a time, beating well after each addition.

Combine the flour, baking powder, lemon zest and salt in a bowl. Add to the butter mixture alternately with the poppy seed mixture, beating until smooth. Pour the batter into a greased 5×9-inch loaf pan.

Bake at 325 degrees for 55 to 60 minutes or until a wooden pick inserted in the center comes out clean. Let cool in the pan on a wire rack.
Yield: 1 loaf.

Make a lemon glaze for the Lemon Poppy Seed Bread by combining sugar and lemon juice in a saucepan over low heat. Cook until the sugar dissolves. Pierce through the loaf of bread about a dozen times with a skewer and pour the hot syrup over the bread. Let cool and wrap in plastic wrap. Let stand for 8 to 10 hours before serving.

Pumpkin Gingerbread

2¹/2 cups unbleached flour
¹/2 cup whole wheat flour
1 cup sugar
1¹/2 teaspoons ginger
1 teaspoon cinnamon
1 teaspoon freshly grated nutmeg
³/4 cup (1¹/2 sticks) unsalted butter, cut into 12 pieces
1 (16-ounce) can pumpkin or 2 cups puréed fresh pumpkin
2 eggs, beaten
¹/2 cup light molasses
¹/3 cup buttermilk
1¹/2 teaspoons baking soda

Combine the unbleached flour and whole wheat flour in a large bowl. Add the sugar, ginger, cinnamon and nutmeg. Cut in the butter with a pastry blender or fork until coarse crumbs form. Reserve ³/4 cup for the topping.

Combine the pumpkin, eggs, molasses, buttermilk and baking soda in a large bowl. Mix well with a whisk. Make a well in the center of the flour mixture. Add the pumpkin mixture and stir just until moistened.

Pour the batter into a greased 9-inch round cake pan. Sprinkle evenly with the reserved crumb topping. Bake at 350 degrees for 40 to 45 minutes or until a wooden pick inserted in the center comes out clean. Let cool in the pan on a wire rack. Serve warm. Yield:12 servings.

Sour Cream Corn Bread

1 cup cornmeal
3 teaspoons baking powder
1 1/2 teaspoons salt
1 cup cream-style corn
2 eggs, lightly beaten
1/2 cup corn oil
1 cup sour cream

Combine the cornmeal, baking powder, salt, corn, eggs, corn oil and sour cream in a large bowl and mix well. Pour into a greased 9×9-inch baking pan. Bake at 400 degrees for 30 minutes or until light brown. This is delicious served with chili or soup. Yield: 8 servings.

Corn Light Bread

1 cup self-rising cornmeal
1 cup flour
1/2 cup sugar
2 teaspoons baking powder
1/4 teaspoon salt
1 1/4 cups buttermilk
1 egg, beaten
1 tablespoon vegetable oil

Combine the cornmeal, flour, sugar, baking powder, salt, buttermilk, egg and oil in a large bowl and mix well. Pour into a large loaf pan. Bake at 425 degrees for 35 to 40 minutes. Yield: 1 loaf.

Jalapeño Corn Bread

1/2 cup flour
1/2 teaspoon salt
1 tablespoon baking powder
1 1/2 cups cornmeal
2 eggs, beaten
1 cup sour cream
1 (8-ounce) can cream-style corn, drained
1/2 cup shortening
1 cup shredded sharp Cheddar cheese
1/2 cup chopped seeded jalapeño peppers

Grease two 8-inch cast-iron skillets and place in a 425-degree oven until very hot. Combine the flour, salt and baking powder in a large bowl. Add the cornmeal and mix well. Stir in the eggs, sour cream, corn, shortening, cheese and peppers. Pour into the prepared skillets. Bake at 425 degrees for 20 to 25 minutes or until golden brown. *Yield: 16 servings.*

Buttermilk Biscuits

2 cups sifted flour
4 teaspoons baking powder
1 teaspoon salt
1/2 teaspoon baking soda
2 tablespoons shortening
1 cup buttermilk
Butter

Sift the flour, baking powder, salt and baking soda into a large bowl. Cut in the shortening with a pastry blender. Add the buttermilk gradually, stirring to form a soft dough. Turn out onto a floured surface. Pat out 1/2 inch thick. Cut with a biscuit cutter and place on a greased baking sheet, sides barely touching. Place a small dab of butter on each biscuit. Bake at 425 degrees for 10 to 15 minutes or until light brown. *Yield: 1 dozen.*

Monkey Bread

3 (10-count) cans refrigerator biscuits
3/4 cup sugar
2 tablespoons cinnamon
1 cup chopped pecans
1/2 cup sugar
1/2 cup packed brown sugar
1/4 cup water
3/4 cup (1 1/2 sticks) butter or margarine
1/2 teaspoon vanilla extract

Cut each biscuit into 6 pieces. Combine 3/4 cup sugar, cinnamon and pecans in a small bowl. Roll each piece of biscuit in the sugar mixture and place in a greased bundt pan.

Combine 1/2 cup sugar, brown sugar, water, butter and vanilla in a saucepan. Bring to a boil and cook until the sugar is dissolved. Pour over the biscuit pieces. Bake at 350 degrees for 30 minutes. Invert onto a serving plate. Pull bread apart to serve. Yield: 10 servings.

Desserts

Sherri Parrish

Sherri Parrish, of Brentwood, Tennessee, believes God has entrusted her with a gift that has manifested itself over many years. She says "because my eyes have been opened in several ways, I see life about me as colorful, vibrant, and exciting… the way He intended. I take this accumulation of joy I see and transform it into a painting." Parrish, who studied at Southern College in Collegedale, Tennessee, works by commission. She says, "If I can add one beautiful thought, a bit of color, or even a little joy to a 'busy world,' then I have found true success."

Shown on overleaf: *Save the Best for Last*

Apple Cake

3 cups chopped apples
2 cups sugar
3/4 cup vegetable oil
2 cups flour
1 teaspoon salt
1 teaspoon baking soda
1 teaspoon cinnamon
1 teaspoon vanilla extract
1 cup chopped pecans (optional)

Combine the apples, sugar and oil in a large bowl. Combine the flour, salt, baking soda and cinnamon in a separate bowl. Add to the apple mixture and mix well. Stir in the vanilla and pecans. Pour into a 9×13-inch cake pan.

Bake at 350 degrees for 30 to 40 minutes. Serve warm with whipped topping or vanilla ice cream. *Yield: 15 servings.*

*Make a delicious **Caramel Frosting** for Apple Cake by melting 1/2 cup (1 stick) butter and 1 cup packed brown sugar in a saucepan. Cook over low heat for 3 minutes, stirring constantly. Add 1/4 cup milk and bring to a boil. Remove from the heat and let cool. Add 2 cups confectioners' sugar and beat well until of spreading consistency.*

Carrot Cake with Cream Cheese Frosting

Cake
2 cups plus 1 tablespoon flour
2 cups sugar
2 teaspoons baking powder
2 teaspoons cinnamon
1 teaspoon baking soda
1 teaspoon salt
1 1/4 cups vegetable oil
4 eggs
2 teaspoons vanilla extract
2 cups grated carrots
1/2 cup chopped pecans

Cream Cheese Frosting
6 ounces cream cheese, softened
3 tablespoons heavy cream
1 1/2 teaspoons vanilla extract
1/2 teaspoon salt
1 (1-pound) package confectioners' sugar
3/4 cup chopped pecans

For the cake, sift the flour, sugar, baking powder, cinnamon, baking soda and salt together in a large mixing bowl. Add the oil and beat for 2 minutes, starting on medium speed and increasing to high speed. Add the eggs and vanilla and beat for 2 minutes. Fold in the carrots and pecans. Pour into two 9-inch round greased and floured cake pans. Bake at 325 degrees for 45 to 50 minutes or until a wooden pick inserted in the center comes out clean. Let cool on wire racks.

For the frosting, combine the cream cheese, cream, vanilla and salt in a mixing bowl. Beat for 5 to 7 minutes or until smooth. Add the confectioners' sugar gradually, beating until of spreading consistency. Fold in the pecans. Spread the frosting between the layers and over the top and side of the cake. Yield: 12 servings.

Chess Cake

$^1/_2$ cup (1 stick) butter
1$^2/_3$ cups packed brown sugar
$^1/_3$ cup sugar
2 eggs
1 cup flour
1 teaspoon baking powder
$^1/_4$ teaspoon salt
1 teaspoon vanilla extract
$^1/_2$ cup chopped pecans
Confectioners' sugar to taste

Melt the butter in a saucepan. Add the brown sugar and sugar and mix well. Cook until the sugar is dissolved, stirring constantly. Add the eggs 1 at time, beating well after each addition. Add the flour, baking powder and salt and mix well. Stir in the vanilla and pecans.

Pour into a greased and floured 8×13-inch cake pan. Bake at 350 degrees for 20 to 25 minutes. Sprinkle the hot cake with confectioners' sugar. Let cool before cutting. *Yield: 15 servings.*

Grandma's Chocolate Cake

Cake

2 cups flour
2 cups sugar
1 teaspoon cinnamon
1/4 teaspoon salt
1/2 cup (1 stick) butter
5 tablespoons baking cocoa
1/2 cup water
1/2 cup cold brewed coffee
1/2 cup vegetable oil
1 teaspoon baking soda
1/2 cup buttermilk
2 eggs, beaten

Chocolate Frosting

1/2 cup (1 stick) butter
4 1/2 tablespoons baking cocoa
6 tablespoons milk
1 (1-pound) package confectioners'
    sugar
1 teaspoon vanilla extract
Chopped pecans (optional)

For the cake, combine the flour, sugar, cinnamon and salt in a large mixing bowl. Set aside. Melt the butter in a saucepan and add the baking cocoa and water and mix well. Remove from the heat and add the coffee and oil and mix well. Add to the flour mixture. Dissolve the baking soda in the buttermilk in a small bowl. Add to the batter along with the eggs and beat for 2 to 3 minutes or until smooth. Pour into a greased and floured 9×13-inch cake pan. Bake at 350 degrees for 25 minutes or until a wooden pick inserted in the center comes out clean.

For the frosting, combine the butter, baking cocoa and milk in a saucepan and bring to a boil. Add the confectioners' sugar and vanilla and beat until smooth. Stir in the pecans. Spread the frosting over the hot cake.
Yield: 15 servings.

Irresistible Grace Cake

1 (2-layer) package yellow cake mix
1 (4-ounce) package chocolate pudding mix
3 eggs
1/3 cup vegetable oil
1 cup sour cream
1 cup (6 ounces) semisweet chocolate chips
1/2 cup (1 stick) butter
1/4 cup baking cocoa
4 to 6 tablespoons brewed coffee
1 (1-pound) package confectioners' sugar

Combine the cake mix, pudding mix, eggs, oil and sour cream in a large mixing bowl and beat until well blended. Stir in the chocolate chips. Pour into a greased and floured bundt pan.

Bake at 375 degrees for 45 minutes. Let cool for 10 minutes. Invert onto a serving plate. Combine the butter, baking cocoa, coffee and confectioners' sugar in a saucepan. Cook until the butter is melted and confectioners' sugar is dissolved, stirring constantly. Pour over the warm cake.
Yield: 16 servings.

Cream of Coconut Cake

1 (2-layer) package white cake mix
1 teaspoon almond extract
1 (14-ounce) can sweetened condensed milk
1 (6-ounce) can cream of coconut
8 ounces whipped topping
1 (3½-ounce) can flaked coconut

Prepare and bake the cake mix according to the package directions for a 9×13-inch cake pan, adding the almond extract. Pierce the hot cake several times with a fork. Combine the sweetened condensed milk and cream of coconut in a bowl and mix well. Pour evenly over the hot cake. Let cool. Spread the whipped topping over the cake and sprinkle with the coconut. Chill until serving time. Yield: 15 *servings*.

Spiced Plum Cake

2 cups sugar
1 cup vegetable oil
3 eggs
3 small jars or 2 large jars plum baby food
1 teaspoon ground cloves
1 teaspoon cinnamon
2 cups self-rising flour

Beat the sugar, oil and eggs in a mixing bowl until well blended. Add the baby food, cloves and cinnamon and mix well. Add the flour and beat until well mixed. Pour into a greased bundt pan. Bake at 350 degrees for 45 to 50 minutes or until a wooden pick inserted in the center comes out clean. Yield: 16 *servings*.

 Try substituting other baby food flavors such as apricot, apple or blueberry in the Spiced Plum Cake. Serve the warm cake with a scoop of vanilla ice cream and drizzle with warm caramel or butterscotch sauce. This cake is sure to become a favorite.

Southern White Chocolate Cake

Cake

1/4 pound white chocolate bark
1 cup (2 sticks) butter, softened
2 cups sugar
4 eggs
2 1/2 cups cake flour
1 teaspoon baking powder
1 teaspoon salt
1 cup buttermilk
1 cup finely chopped pecans
1 (3 1/2-ounce) can flaked coconut
1 teaspoon coconut extract
1 teaspoon almond extract

White Chocolate Icing

1/4 pound white chocolate bark, almost
  melted
1 cup sugar
1/2 cup (1 stick) butter, softened
1/4 cup evaporated milk
1 tablespoon light corn syrup
1/4 teaspoon coconut extract
1/4 teaspoon almond extract
1/8 teaspoon salt
12 (or more) miniature marshmallows

For the cake, melt the white chocolate over boiling water in a double boiler. Beat the butter, sugar and melted chocolate in a large mixing bowl until light and well blended. Add the eggs 1 a time, beating for 1 minute after each addition. Combine the flour, baking powder and salt in a separate bowl. Add the flour mixture alternately with the buttermilk, beating well after each addition. Fold in the pecans, coconut, coconut extract and almond extract. Pour into a greased and floured bundt pan. Bake at 350 degrees for 1 hour. Let cool and invert onto a serving plate.

For the icing, combine the white chocolate, sugar, butter, evaporated milk, corn syrup, coconut extract, almond extract and salt in a saucepan and mix well. Let stand for 1 hour, stirring occasionally. Cook over medium heat until a soft ball forms when dropped from a spoon. Add the marshmallows and stir until melted. Remove from the heat and let cool. Beat until of spreading consistency. Spread the icing over the warm cake. Yield: 16 servings.

Buttermilk Pound Cake

¹/₂ teaspoon baking soda
1 tablespoon boiling water
1 cup (2 sticks) butter, softened
3 cups sugar
5 eggs
3 cups flour
1 cup buttermilk
2 teaspoons vanilla extract

Dissolve the baking soda in the boiling water in a small bowl. Cream the butter and sugar in a large mixing bowl until light and fluffy. Add the eggs 1 at a time, beating well after each addition. Add the flour, baking soda mixture, buttermilk and vanilla and beat until well blended.

Pour the batter into a greased tube or bundt pan. Bake at 350 degrees for 1¹/₂ hours. Serve with a scoop of vanilla ice cream and fresh fruit.
Yield: *16 servings.*

 Make 4 pound cakes in one. Prepare 4 different flavors of pound cakes such as lemon, marble, cream cheese, orange, or chocolate chip in bundt pans. Cut the cakes into quarters and reassemble on a cake plate. Freeze until needed or give as a gift.

Buckeyes

1 pound creamy peanut butter
2 cups (4 sticks) margarine, softened
3 (1-pound) packages confectioners' sugar
1 bar paraffin
2 cups (12 ounces) semisweet chocolate chips

Combine the peanut butter, margarine and confectioners' sugar in a large bowl and mix until well blended. Shape into 1-inch balls. Chill, covered, for 1 hour or longer. Melt the paraffin and chocolate chips in a double boiler. Dip the peanut butter balls into the chocolate mixture with a wooden pick, turning to coat well. Place on waxed paper to cool until firm. Store in an airtight container in the refrigerator. These make great gifts to give to anyone, especially during the holidays. *Yield*: 100.

Cracker Candy

40 saltine crackers
1 cup (2 sticks) butter
1 cup packed brown sugar
2 cups (12 ounces) milk chocolate chips

Line the crackers side by side on a foil-lined baking pan. Combine the butter and brown sugar in a saucepan. Bring to a boil and cook for 3 minutes, stirring constantly. Pour evenly over the crackers. Bake at 400 degrees for 5 minutes. Sprinkle the chocolate chips over the hot crackers.

Let stand for 5 minutes for the chocolate chips to melt. Spread the melted chocolate evenly over the top. Chill, covered, until firm. Invert onto waxed paper; remove the foil. Break into pieces. Store in an airtight container in the refrigerator. *Yield*: 24 *servings*.

Miss Bonnie's Cookies

1 cup rolled oats
3/4 cup butter-flavored shortening
1 1/4 cups packed brown sugar
1 egg
2 tablespoons milk
1 tablespoon vanilla extract
2 cups flour
1 teaspoon salt
3/4 teaspoon baking soda
2 cups (12 ounces) chocolate chips

Process the oats in a blender until finely ground. Cream the shortening and brown sugar in a mixing bowl until light and fluffy. Add the egg, milk and vanilla and beat until well blended. Add the ground oats, flour, salt and baking soda and mix well. Fold in the chocolate chips. Shape the dough into 1-inch balls. Place on a cookie sheet. Bake at 375 degrees for 8 minutes. Yield: 2 dozen.

Kim's Chocolate Chip Cookies

1 cup (2 sticks) margarine, softened
1 cup packed brown sugar
1/2 cup sugar
2 eggs
2 teaspoons vanilla extract
1 cup rolled oats
2 1/4 cups flour
1 teaspoon baking soda
2 cups (12 ounces) semisweet chocolate chips

Combine the margarine, brown sugar and sugar in a large bowl and mix well with a spoon. Stir in the eggs and vanilla. Add the oats and mix well. Add the flour and baking soda and mix well. Fold in the chocolate chips. Drop by spoonfuls onto cookie sheets. Bake at 350 degrees for 10 minutes. Yield: 2 dozen.

Butter Cookies

1 cup (2 sticks) butter, softened
3/4 cup sugar
1 egg
1/2 teaspoon vanilla extract
2 1/2 cups flour
1 teaspoon baking powder
1/4 teaspoon salt

Cream the butter and sugar in a mixing bowl until light and fluffy. Add the egg and vanilla and beat well. Combine the flour, baking powder and salt in a bowl. Add to the creamed mixture and mix well. Roll out on a floured surface and cut with a cookie cutter. You may also press the dough through a cookie press. Place on cookie sheets. Bake at 350 degrees for 10 to 12 minutes. Do not substitute margarine for the butter. *Yield: 3 dozen.*

Date Nut Cookies

1 teaspoon baking soda
4 teaspoons hot water
1 cup (2 sticks) butter, softened
2 cups packed brown sugar
2 eggs
1 teaspoon baking powder

1 teaspoon cinnamon
1/2 teaspoon salt
1 teaspoon vanilla extract
1 cup chopped pecans
1 cup chopped dried dates
4 cups flour

Dissolve the baking soda in the hot water in a small bowl. Beat the butter and brown sugar in a mixing bowl until light and fluffy. Beat in the eggs. Add the baking powder, cinnamon and salt and mix well. Add the baking soda mixture and vanilla and beat until well blended. Stir in the pecans and dates. Add the flour gradually, mixing well.

Separate into 3 or 4 equal portions. Shape into logs and wrap in waxed paper. Chill until firm. Cut into thin slices and place on cookie sheets. Bake at 450 degrees for 10 minutes. *Yield: 3 to 4 dozen.*

Gingerbread Cookies

2 cups packed brown sugar
1 1/2 cups (3 sticks) butter, softened
1 egg
4 cups flour
2 teaspoons cinnamon
1 teaspoon nutmeg
1/2 teaspoon cloves
1/4 teaspoon baking soda

Cream the brown sugar and butter in a mixing bowl until light and fluffy. Beat in the egg. Combine the flour, cinnamon, nutmeg, cloves and baking soda in a large bowl. Add to the creamed mixture and mix well. Chill the dough, covered, for 2 hours. Roll out to 1/8-inch thickness. Cut out with desired cookie cutters. Place on cookie sheets. Bake at 350 degrees for 8 to 10 minutes. Yield: 4 dozen.

 These make great cookies to decorate around the holidays. Use store-bought frosting in all colors along with colored sugars and other candy sprinkles to personalize your cookies. They don't just have to be gingerbread people, either. Try other cookies cutters in the shapes of trees, ornaments, bells, and stars. This is an afternoon of fun for children of all ages.

Wedding Cookies

1 cup (2 sticks) butter or margarine, softened
3/4 cup sugar
2 teaspoons water
2 teaspoons vanilla extract
2 cups flour
1 cup chopped pecans
Confectioners' sugar

Cream the butter and sugar in a mixing bowl until light and fluffy. Add the water and vanilla and beat until well blended. Add the flour and pecans and mix well. Chill, covered, for 1 hour. Shape into small balls and place on cookie sheets. Bake at 375 degrees for 10 minutes. Let cool slightly and roll in confectioners' sugar. Yield: 5 dozen.

Butterscotch Brownies

2 cups flour
2 teaspoons baking powder
1½ teaspoons salt
2 cups (12 ounces) butterscotch chips
½ cup (1 stick) margarine

2 cups packed brown sugar
4 eggs
1 teaspoon vanilla extract
1 cup chopped pecans

Combine the flour, baking powder and salt in a large bowl; set aside. Melt the butterscotch chips and margarine in a saucepan. Remove from the heat and pour into another large bowl. Add the brown sugar and stir until well blended. Let cool for 5 minutes. Beat in the eggs and vanilla. Add the flour mixture gradually, stirring until well blended. Stir in the pecans. Spread into a greased 10×15-inch baking pan. Bake at 350 degrees for 30 minutes. Let cool and cut into squares. *Yield: 2 dozen.*

German Coffee Bars

1 cup packed brown sugar
¼ cup shortening
1 egg
½ cup hot brewed coffee
1½ cups flour
1 teaspoon baking powder

½ teaspoon cinnamon
¼ teaspoon baking soda
¼ teaspoon salt
¼ teaspoon ginger
¼ teaspoon cloves
½ cup raisins

Beat the brown sugar, shortening and egg in a mixing bowl until well blended. Stir in the coffee. Combine the flour, baking powder, cinnamon, baking soda, salt, ginger and cloves in a bowl. Add to the brown sugar mixture gradually, beating until well blended. Fold in the raisins.

Spread into a greased 9×12-inch baking pan. Bake at 350 degrees for 30 minutes. Let cool and cut into squares to serve. You may frost with a buttercream frosting while warm if desired. *Yield: 15 bars.*

Buttermilk Pie

1 1/2 cups sugar
1 tablespoon flour
1/2 cup (1 stick) butter or margarine,
    melted

3 eggs, beaten
1/4 cup buttermilk
1 unbaked (9-inch) pie shell
Chopped pecans (optional)

Combine the sugar and flour in a bowl. Pour the melted butter over the sugar mixture and mix well. Add the eggs and buttermilk and mix well. Pour into the pie shell. Sprinkle with the chopped pecans. Bake at 350 degrees for 1 hour. This pie freezes well. *Yield: 6 to 8 servings.*

Grasshopper Pie

36 chocolate wafers
1/3 cup butter, melted
1 envelope unflavored gelatin
1/2 cup cold water
1/3 cup sugar
1/8 teaspoon salt
3 egg yolks, beaten

1/4 cup crème de menthe
1/4 cup white crème de cacao
3 egg whites
1/3 cup sugar
1 cup whipping cream
Chocolate wafer crumbs

Process the wafers and melted butter in a blender until crumbly. Press over the bottom and up the side of a springform pan. Chill the crust until ready to use.

Sprinkle the gelatin over the cold water, 1/3 cup sugar, salt and egg yolks in a saucepan. Cook over low heat just until the mixture begins to boil. Remove from the heat and stir in the crème de menthe and crème de cacao. Chill for 20 to 30 minutes or until partially set.

Beat the egg whites in a mixing bowl until soft peaks form. Add 1/3 cup sugar gradually, beating until stiff peaks form. Fold into the gelatin mixture. Beat the whipping cream in a mixing bowl until soft peaks form and fold into the mixture. Pour into the prepared crust. Top with chocolate wafer crumbs. Chill for several hours before serving. *Yield: 8 to 10 servings.*

Chocolate Pie

1/4 cup baking cocoa
1 cup sugar
2 tablespoons flour
1/4 teaspoon salt
1 cup milk
4 egg yolks, beaten

1/4 cup (1/2 stick) butter
1 teaspoon vanilla extract
1 baked (9-inch) pie shell
4 egg whites
1/2 cup sugar

Combine the baking cocoa, 1 cup sugar, flour and salt in a heavy saucepan. Add the milk and cook over low heat just until the mixture begins to boil, stirring constantly. Remove from the heat; do not bring to a full boil. Add a small amount of the hot mixture to the beaten egg yolks in a bowl and mix well. Repeat this 8 times. Spoon the egg yolk mixture into the hot baking cocoa mixture and pour into a double boiler. Cook until thickened, stirring frequently. Add the butter and vanilla. Cook until the butter is melted, stirring constantly. Pour into the pie shell.

Beat the egg whites in a mixing bowl until soft peaks form. Add 1/2 cup sugar gradually, beating until stiff peaks form. Spread the meringue over the pie, sealing to the edge. Bake at 350 degrees for 10 minutes or until light brown. *Yield: 6 to 8 servings.*

Sinful Chocolate Caramel Pie

1/2 cup chopped pecans
1 (9-inch) graham cracker pie shell
17 caramel squares
1/4 cup evaporated milk
2 cups (12 ounces) semisweet
    chocolate chips

1/4 cup (1/2 stick) butter or margarine
1 1/3 cups heavy cream
Whipped topping

Place the pecans in the bottom of the pie shell. Melt the caramels with the evaporated milk in a double boiler, stirring constantly. Pour over the pecans. Melt the chocolate chips and butter with the cream in a double boiler. Cook until thickened, stirring constantly. Pour over the caramel mixture in the pie shell. Chill until set. Dollop with whipped topping before serving. *Yield: 8 servings.*

Fresh Peach Pie

1 1/3 cups sugar
1/4 cup cornstarch
1/8 teaspoon salt
1 1/3 cups water
1/3 cup apricot gelatin
1/2 teaspoon almond extract
1 tablespoon lemon juice
4 cups chopped fresh peaches
2 baked (10-inch) deep-dish pie shells
Whipped topping
Nutmeg to taste

Combine the sugar, cornstarch, salt and water in a saucepan. Cook until thickened, stirring constantly. Remove from the heat. Stir in the gelatin, almond extract and lemon juice. Chill until partially set. Fold in the peaches. Spoon into the 2 pie shells. Chill until set. Serve with whipped topping and sprinkle with nutmeg. You may substitute orange or peach gelatin for the apricot. *Yield: 12 servings.*

Basic Pie Crust

1 2/3 cups flour
1 teaspoon salt
3/4 cup shortening
1/3 cup flour
1/4 cup ice water

Combine 1 2/3 cups flour and salt in a bowl. Cut in the shortening until coarse crumbs form. Combine 1/3 cup flour and the ice water in a bowl, mixing to form a paste. Add the paste mixture to the crumb mixture. Stir just until mixed. Shape into a ball. Let rest, covered, for 5 minutes. Roll out onto a pastry cloth or waxed paper. Divide into 2 portions. Fit into pie plates and prick with a fork. *Yield: 2 pie shells.*

Frozen Peanut Butter Pie

3 ounces cream cheese, softened
1 cup sifted confectioners' sugar
1/3 cup plus 2 tablespoons creamy peanut butter
1/2 cup milk
9 ounces whipped topping
1 (9-inch) graham cracker pie shell
1/4 cup finely chopped peanuts

Beat the cream cheese in a mixing bowl until light and fluffy. Add the confectioners' sugar and peanut butter and beat at medium speed until well blended. Add the milk gradually, beating until well mixed. Fold in the whipped topping. Spoon into the pie shell. Sprinkle with the peanuts. Freeze until firm. *Yield: 6 to 8 servings.*

Pecan Pie

1/2 cup sugar
2/3 cup packed brown sugar
3 eggs, lightly beaten
1/2 cup (1 stick) butter, melted
1/2 cup light corn syrup
1/2 cup dark corn syrup
1 1/2 teaspoons vanilla extract
1 cup coarsely chopped pecans
1 unbaked (9-inch) pie shell

Combine the sugar, brown sugar and eggs in a large bowl and mix until light and fluffy. Add the melted butter, light corn syrup, dark corn syrup and vanilla and mix well. Stir in the pecans. Pour into the pie shell. Bake at 350 degrees for 1 hour. Let cool for 1 hour before slicing. *Yield: 8 servings.*

Banana Pudding

³/₄ cup sugar
¹/₃ cup flour or 3 tablespoons
    cornstarch
¹/₄ teaspoon salt
2 cups milk
3 egg yolks
2 tablespoons butter

1 teaspoon vanilla extract
1 box vanilla wafers
3 to 4 bananas, sliced
3 egg whites
¹/₂ teaspoon vanilla extract
¹/₄ teaspoon cream of tartar
6 tablespoons sugar

Combine ³/₄ cup sugar, flour and salt in a saucepan and mix well. Stir in the milk gradually. Cook over medium heat until mixture begins to boil, stirring constantly. Cook for 2 minutes, stirring constantly. Remove from the heat.

Beat the egg yolks in a small bowl. Stir a small amount of the hot mixture into the egg yolks. Add the egg yolk mixture to the hot mixture. Cook for 2 minutes over medium heat, stirring constantly. Remove from the heat. Stir in the butter and 1 teaspoon vanilla.

Arrange 1 layer of vanilla wafers in the bottom of a 2- or 3-quart baking dish. Top with 1 layer of sliced bananas. Pour half of the prepared pudding over the layer of bananas. Repeat the layers of vanilla wafers and bananas. Top with the remaining pudding.

Beat the egg whites with ¹/₂ teaspoon vanilla and cream of tartar in a mixing bowl until soft peaks form. Add 6 tablespoons sugar gradually, beating until stiff peaks form. Spread the meringue over the top of the pudding, sealing to the edge. Bake at 350 degrees for 12 to 15 minutes or until light brown. Let cool before serving. *Yield: 8 servings.*

 Try using the Banana Pudding as a delicious filling for crepes. For a lighter texture, fold in 1 to 2 cups whipped cream and add banana slices. Spoon into prepared crepes and drizzle with a warm caramel sauce. Sprinkle with toasted pecans for a delicious dessert.

Creamy Cheesecake

1 2/3 cups graham cracker crumbs
2 tablespoons sugar
1/2 teaspoon cinnamon
6 tablespoons butter, melted
24 ounces cream cheese, softened
1 cup sugar

3 eggs
1/2 teaspoon vanilla extract
1 cup sour cream
3 tablespoons sugar
1/2 teaspoon vanilla extract

Combine the graham cracker crumbs, 2 tablespoons sugar, cinnamon and melted butter in a bowl and mix well. Press over the bottom and up the side of a springform pan. Beat the cream cheese in a mixing bowl until light and fluffy. Add 1 cup sugar, eggs and 1/2 teaspoon vanilla and beat well. Pour into the prepared crust. Bake at 375 degrees for 20 minutes. Combine the sour cream, 3 tablespoons sugar, and 1/2 teaspoon vanilla in a bowl and mix well. Pour over the baked layer. Bake at 500 degrees for 5 minutes. Chill until serving time. Yield: 12 *servings*.

Mocha Cheesecake Savanno

1 cup flour
1/4 cup sugar
Grated zest of 1 lemon
1 egg yolk
1/2 cup (1 stick) butter, softened
40 ounces cream cheese, softened

1 1/2 cups sugar
1/4 cup flour
1/4 teaspoon salt
6 eggs
2 tablespoons instant coffee granules
1/3 cup amaretto

Combine 1 cup flour, 1/4 cup sugar and lemon zest in a large bowl. Add the egg yolk and butter and mix well with your fingers until a smooth dough forms. Shape into a ball, wrap in plastic wrap and chill for 1 hour. Roll the dough out on a floured surface and press over the bottom and up the side of a 9-inch springform pan. Beat the cream cheese in a large mixing bowl until light and fluffy. Beat in 1 1/2 cups sugar, 1/4 cup flour and salt. Add the eggs 1 at a time, beating well after each addition. Dissolve the coffee granules into the amaretto in a bowl. Add to the creamed mixture and mix well. Spoon into the prepared pan. Bake at 250 degrees for 2 to 3 hours or until the center is set. Let cool. Chill until serving time. Garnish with almond slivers, strawberries or chocolate shavings. You may also top with whipped cream and sprinkle with instant coffee granules. Yield: 16 *servings*.

Tiramisu

6 egg yolks
1/2 cup plus 1 tablespoon sugar
8 ounces mascarpone cheese
1 1/2 cups whipping cream, whipped
6 cups very strong brewed coffee
2 packages ladyfingers
Baking cocoa
Confectioners' sugar

Whisk the egg yolks and sugar in a double boiler. Cook until thick and pale yellow and 140 degrees on a candy thermometer. Remove from the heat and let cool. Whisk in the mascarpone cheese until smooth and thickened. Fold in the whipped cream. Spread a thin layer in the bottom of a 12×16-inch dish. Pour the coffee into a small bowl. Lightly dip the ladyfingers in the coffee. Arrange the prepared ladyfingers over the top of the mascarpone cheese layer.

Spread a layer of the mascarpone mixture over the top of the ladyfingers. Top with another layer of ladyfingers that have been lightly dipped in the coffee. Top with the remaining mascarpone mixture. Chill, covered, for 3 to 4 hours before serving. Sprinkle with baking cocoa and confectioners' sugar before serving. *Yield: 10 to 12 servings.*

Summer Fruit Crisp

Filling
1 cup sugar
1 cup water
1/4 cup cornstarch
2 teaspoons fresh lemon juice
1 teaspoon vanilla extract
4 cups chopped rhubarb (fresh or
    frozen)
1 cup strawberries, hulled, quartered
3/4 cup blueberries
1 1/2 teaspoons grated orange zest

Topping
1/2 cup rolled oats
3/4 cup flour
3/4 cup packed brown sugar
6 tablespoons butter, melted
1 teaspoon cinnamon

For the filling, combine the sugar, water and cornstarch in a medium saucepan. Cook over medium heat until thickened and clear, stirring constantly. Remove from the heat and stir in the lemon juice and vanilla. Fold in the rhubarb, strawberries, blueberries and orange zest. Spoon into an 8- or 9-inch baking dish.

For the topping, combine the oats, flour, brown sugar, melted butter and cinnamon in a bowl and mix well until crumbly. Sprinkle evenly over the filling.

Bake at 350 degrees for 45 to 55 minutes or until bubbly. Serve warm with whipped cream or vanilla ice cream. Yield: 6 to 8 servings.

Fruit Pizza

Crust
1 cup (2 sticks) butter, softened
1 1/2 cups sugar
2 eggs
1 tablespoon almond extract
1/2 teaspoon vanilla extract
3 cups flour
1 teaspoon baking powder
1 teaspoon baking soda

Topping
16 ounces cream cheese, softened
Banana slices
Red and green grape halves
Plum slices
Raspberries
Peach slices
Blueberries
Kiwifruit slices
Pear slices
2 cups apricot preserves

For *the crust*, cream the butter and sugar in a large mixing bowl until light and fluffy. Add the eggs and beat well. Add the almond extract and vanilla and mix well. Add the flour, baking powder and baking soda and mix until a dough forms. Pat the dough into a 16-inch round pizza pan. Bake at 350 degrees for 15 minutes or until light brown. Let cool.

For *the topping*, spread the cream cheese over the baked crust. Arrange the fruit over the cream cheese in a decorative pattern. Heat the apricot preserves in a microwave-safe bowl in the microwave until heated through. Drizzle the warm preserves over the top. Cut into squares or slices to serve. Yield: *16 servings*.

For a timesaver, use refrigerator sugar cookie dough for the crust of the Fruit Pizza. You may make your own sauce by combining 1 tablespoon cornstarch, 1/4 cup sugar, 1 teaspoon lemon juice and 1/2 cup apple juice. Drizzle over the fruit in place of the apricot preserves.

Butterscotch Crepes

Dessert Crepes
4 eggs
1 cup flour
2 tablespoons sugar
1 cup milk
1/4 cup water
1 tablespoon unsalted butter, melted

Butterscotch Mousse Filling
1 (4-ounce) package butterscotch
   cook-and-serve pudding
1 cup whipping cream, whipped

Warm Caramel Sauce
3/4 cup plus 2 tablespoons sugar
3 tablespoons cold water
2 cups heavy cream
1 teaspoon vanilla extract
1 1/2 teaspoons cold unsalted butter

Assembly
Toasted chopped pecans
Whipped cream

For the crepes, combine the eggs, flour, sugar, milk, water and melted butter in a blender container. Process for 1 minute. Scrape sides of blender and process for 15 seconds or until smooth. Chill, covered, for 1 hour or longer. Heat a 7- or 8-inch crepe pan and brush with additional butter. Spoon 2 to 3 tablespoons of the crepe batter into the pan for each crepe and tilt the pan to cover evenly. Cook over medium heat for 1 to 2 minutes or until golden brown. Remove the crepes to a plate.

For the filling, prepare the pudding according to the package directions. Fold in the whipped cream.

For the sauce, combine the sugar and cold water in a saucepan. Cook over medium heat until the sugar dissolves, stirring constantly and scraping down the side of the pan. Bring to a boil and cook for 5 to 10 minutes or until the mixture caramelizes; do not stir. Remove from the heat and add the cream gradually, being careful not to let the mixture bubble up. Bring to a gentle boil over medium heat. Cook for 5 to 6 minutes or until thickened. Remove from the heat and stir in the vanilla and butter.

To assemble, spoon 2 to 3 spoonfuls of the Butterscotch Mousse Filling into each Dessert Crepe. Fold the crepe lengthwise and seal the edges. Place seam side down on a dessert plate. Drizzle with the Warm Caramel Sauce. Sprinkle with toasted chopped pecans and a spoonful of whipped cream. Yield: 20 servings.

Homemade Vanilla Ice Cream

6 eggs
2 cups sugar
1 (12-ounce) can evaporated milk
2 (14-ounce) cans sweetened condensed milk
1 tablespoon vanilla extract
Whole milk
2 bags ice
1 box rock salt

Beat the eggs in a mixing bowl for 5 minutes. Add the sugar gradually, beating until thick and pale yellow. Add the evaporated milk and sweetened condensed milk and beat well. Mix in the vanilla. Pour into an ice cream freezer container. Add milk to the fill line. Alternate ice and rock salt and freeze using the manufacturer's directions. *Yield: Variable.*

 To avoid raw eggs that may carry salmonella, use the equivalent amount of pasteurized egg substitute.

Homemade Chocolate Ice Cream

1 (16-ounce) can Hershey's chocolate syrup
1/2 cup whole milk
10 large marshmallows
2 cups sugar
4 cups half-and-half
1 tablespoon vanilla extract
2 cups heavy cream

Combine the chocolate syrup and milk in a saucepan. Cook over medium heat, stirring constantly. Add the marshmallows and cook until melted, stirring constantly. Add the sugar and cook until dissolved, stirring constantly. Stir in the half-and-half and vanilla. Remove from the heat and stir in the cream. Pour into an ice cream freezer container. Freeze using the manufacturer's directions. *Yield: 20 servings.*

Cookbook Committee

Anne McDow Keener '91

Melissa McCall

Nikki Brock Wright '80

Anne Gillem

Leah Hoskins

Nancy Holyfield

Dori Howard

Contributors List

Millie Abner
Linda Adair
Nan Adams
Dawn Adcock
Stacy Allen
Wyatt Allen
Jo Anderson
Kathy Anderson
Laura Anderson
Stacey Richardson Andrews
Renee Ard
Mary Armistead
Lori Wells Arrington
Brent Atema
Carol Atema

Vicki Innis Atnip
Harriet Brown Bailey
Mary Baker
Jennifer White Barnes
Amy Wadlington Bayles
Beth Beasley
Ryan Benefield
Lyn Berry
Ellie Billington
Ian Black
Paula Blanton
Linda Bliss
Melissa Bloemer
Anne Boling
Marcia Bowen

Lynne Bowers
Pamela Bowker
Chelsea Brock
Darlene Brock
Nancy Brock
Penny Brooks
Anna Brown
Bill Brown
Julie Brown
Lee Russell Brown
Debby Bryan
Heather Husband Buffkin
Carol Watkins Bumbalough
Alice Burcham
Cindi Burger

Diane Burke
Laura Burkhart
Mary Ruth Cameron
Elizabeth Cantrell
Cheryl Chamberlain
Kalpana Gowda
   Chandrashkar
Julie Chukas
Lulu Luton Clark
Karmen Clift
Jane Cohea
Lu Cole
Terri Delboy Coley
Jeanie Collier
Angie Curtis Collins
Michelle Cowan
Carla Cox
Pearl Cox
Marsha Crownover
Jan Rodgers Dale
Heidi Bihun Dennison
Bonnie Bennett Dixon
Norma Dodson
Margaret Dye
Laura Eddleman
Anne Adams Edmonds
Ginger Edwards
Nora Edwards
April Eshelman
Pam Evins
Cynthia Ezell
Lynda Fadler
Brendan Finucane
Shannon Finucane
Judy Flatt
Karen Gant Forehand

Debbie Forte
George Fusner
Myra Fusner
Linda Fuson
Bonni Futch
Kay Kephart Galloway
Donna Garrett
Sue Gering
Anne Gillem
Judy Goodman
Missy Goodman
Brad Greer
Amy Skaggs Harr
Amy Heimermann
Dana Hessey
Carolyn Hill
DeeAnn Booth Hodge
Brenda Holmes
Nancy Holyfield
Chris Hoover
Leah Hoskins
Teresa Houk
Laurie Hays Houston
Dorie Howard
Melinda Howser
Danielle Faris Hulgan
Doris Webb Jackson
Natalie Peek Jackson
Charmaine Jamieson
Walls Janet
Ellen Jewell
Debbie Jocobs
Kathy Petty Jones
Margaret Jordan
Susan Joseph
Dave Kempf

Marie Kephart
Lyn Kerns
Tina Kester
Valerie Battle Kienzle
Janie Kincaid
Rachel Clift Knox
Myleen Kottas
Lindy Lawrence
Jeanie Leim
Sallie Lewis
Ann Linebaugh
Betty Little
Lisa Littlejohn
Mary Logan
Sarah Lundy
Eddie & Jordan Lunn
Milah Lynn
Matt MacIntyre
Sabrina Maggart
Libby Marley
Julie Mason
Cindy Masters
Diane Mayfield
Lois Reeves McAlister
Molly & Andy McAllester
Melissa McCall
Billie McCollum
Linda McDavitt
Carla McDougle
Jane McDow
Katherine McDowell
Brittany McGowan
Roxanne McGowan
Jan McKaskle
Mary Beth McNamara
Sheran Townsend McNatt

Cleatrice McTorry	Jane Richards	Kim Stewart
Jan Meek	Jamie Riggs	Adora Swanson
Clara Miller	Susan Riggs	Barbara Taylor
Betty Anne Mills	Sheila Roberts	Donna Taylor
Paige Waldrop Mills	Caryn Robinson	Marcy Thomas
Ann Armistead Moore	Ross Robinson	Trina Thomas
Polly Moore	Honey Rodgers	Chris Thorpe
Catherine Morris	Molly Edmondson Rollins	Connie Thurman
Julie Morris	Mary Lea Roselle	Pia Rooth Tinsley
Nancy Morrison	Joann Rosenbaum	Nancy Cartwright Tirrill
Kathy Moult	Lynn Rutledge	Melodie Tunney
Michelle Mountain	Debbie Krauth Sanders	Jenny Hicks Valle
Victoria Mueller	Sharon Sanders	Janie Varn
Gwen Mullican	Belinda Schmidt	Julia Vaughn
Judy Murchison	Susan Schmitter	Lyn Walker
Ellen Murphree	Betsy Seckman	Marrie Walker
Sharon Murphy	Caren Shaffer	Thomas Walker
Lana Hadden Myers	Debbie Shaw	Janet Walls
Becky & Aubrey Naish	Jean Sheriff	Mae Ann Watson
Laurie Nebel	Ann Paige Shull	Heidi Huebner Weimer
Helen Neese	Livy Sibley	Tammi Wells
Laura Newton	Lynn Simpson	Julie West
Debbie Oaks	Melinda Simpson	Monica West
Tam Tillman Owen	Linda Skaggs	Cammie Cherry White
Jennifer Smith Ozburn	Mandy Skaggs	Pat Whitson
Cathy Parkey	Sharyn Slaughter	Ann Williams
Gwen Patrick	Barbara Smith	Lauraie Williams
Lisa Patrick	Carolyn Smith	Richmond Williams
Nancy Pelster	Jane Smith	Pamela Willis
Sandy Pizzini	Karen Smith	Marie Willoughby
Sara Posthuma	Peggie Smith	Connie Wilson
Cayce Burke Price	Ann Smithson	Courtney Rudolph Wilson
Lynn Queener	Carol Solesby	Shawn Wilson
Aggie Read	Pam Speedy	Deborah Wyatt
Neely Reddick	Debbie Sperring	Pam Wylly
Lynn Beasley Rhoades	Stephanie Staniewski	Joann Young

Index

Appetizers. *See also* Dips;
Snacks; Spreads
Barbecue Basil Shrimp, 40
Cheddar Cheese Toast, 42
Chicken and Brie
Quesadillas, 36
Crab Cakes, 39
Crab Swiss Bites, 39
Favorite Party Pork
Tenderloins, 38
Marinated Asparagus, 35
Marinated Wild Duck
Breasts, 130
Spinach Roll, 37
Thai Shrimp, 41
Apple
Apple Cake, 161
Baked Butternut Squash, 17
Brown's Breakfast, 65
Festive Fruit Salad, 83
Winter Fruit Salad with
Lemon Poppy Seed
Dressing, 86
Artichokes
Caviar Artichokes, 12
Chicken Artichoke Soup, 77
Cold Artichoke Dip, 31
Roasted Red Bell Pepper and
Artichoke Dip, 30
Spinach Artichoke
Casserole, 101
Asparagus
Asparagus Salad, 80
Marinated Asparagus, 35
Seaside Pasta, 138
Bacon
Broccoli and Bacon Salad, 80
Fourth of July Bean
Casserole, 92
Swiss Bacon Dip, 32
Banana
Apricot Salad, 84
Banana Bread, 152
Banana Pudding, 178
Bread Machine Banana
Granola Bread, 146
Brown's Breakfast, 65
Chocolate Chip Banana
Bread, 153
Festive Fruit Salad, 83
Fruit Pizza, 182
Beans. *See also* Green Beans
Black Bean Salsa, 29

Chili for a Crowd, 79
Fourth of July Bean
Casserole, 92
Téjas Chili, 79
West African Red Beans and
Rice, 121
White Bean Chili, 20
Working Barn Stew, 78
Beef. *See also* Ground Beef
Barbecue Flank Steak, 110
Beef Tenderloin, 109
Chinese Pepper Steak, 111
Three-Day Brisket, 109
Beverages, Cold. *See also*
Smoothies
Almond Punch, 68
Carrot Cooler, 67
Cranberry Tea, 70
Ginger Tea, 26
Pink Lady Punch, 69
Punch for a Crowd, 69
Beverages, Hot
Apricot Nectar Hot Punch, 66
Hot Cranberry Mull, 67
Hot Spiced Percolator
Punch, 68
Wassail Punch, 18
Blueberry
Blueberry Coffee Cake, 58
Festive Fruit Salad, 83
Fruit Pizza, 182
Oatmeal Blueberry Muffins, 63
Summer Fruit Crisp, 181
Breads. *See also* Coffee Cakes;
Corn Bread; Muffins;
Pancakes
Buttermilk Biscuits, 157
Cheddar Cheese Toast, 42
Double-Orange Scones, 64
Monkey Bread, 158
Pumpkin Gingerbread, 155
Breads, Loaves
Almond Poppy Seed
Bread, 150
Banana Bread, 152
Chocolate Chip Banana
Bread, 153
Dried Apricot Pecan
Bread, 151
Lemon Poppy Seed Bread, 154
Breads, Yeast
Bread Machine Banana
Granola Bread, 146

Bread Machine Honey Wheat
Bread, 147
Cranberry Oatmeal Nut
Bread, 143
Dilly Bread, 144
Feta Cheese Bread, 145
Light Whole Wheat
Bread, 148
Refrigerator Rolls, 149
Soft Pretzels, 44
Whole Wheat Rolls, 149
Brie
Baked Brie with Cranberry
Chutney, 12
Chicken and Brie
Quesadillas, 36
Broccoli
Broccoli and Bacon Salad, 80
Broccoli Casserole, 93
Tri-Colored Vegetable Pasta
Salad, 81
Brunch
Crunchy Granola, 65
Double-Orange Scones, 64
Nana's Cheese Grits, 53
Butters/Rubs
Honey Butter Spread, 56
Maple Herb Butter, 16
Zesty Orange Rub for
Pork, 120
Cakes
Apple Cake, 161
Buttermilk Pound
Cake, 168
Carrot Cake with Cream
Cheese Frosting, 162
Chess Cake, 163
Cream of Coconut Cake, 166
Grandma's Chocolate
Cake, 164
Irresistible Grace Cake, 165
Pumpkin Gingerbread, 155
Southern White Chocolate
Cake, 167
Spiced Plum Cake, 166
Candy
Buckeyes, 169
Cracker Candy, 169
Carrots
Carrot Cake with Cream
Cheese Frosting, 162
Carrot Cooler, 67
Cheese Soup, 76

Copper Pennies, 93
Tri-Colored Vegetable Pasta
    Salad, 81
Cheesecakes
Creamy Cheesecake, 179
Mocha Cheesecake
    Savanno, 179
Chicken
Algerian Chicken, 25
Chicken and Brie
    Quesadillas, 36
Chicken Artichoke Soup, 77
Chicken Bundles, 125
Chicken Potpie, 127
Chicken with Fruited Wild
    Rice, 124
Company Chicken
    Casserole, 126
Crispy Chicken Breast, 123
Gulf Shrimp Newspaper
    Dinner, 135
Homemade Chicken Noodle
    Soup, 77
Hot Chicken Salad, 125
Linguine with Chicken,
    Sun-Dried Tomatoes and
    Gorgonzola, 129
Sesame Baked Chicken, 122
Spicy African Chicken
    Stew, 128
Sweet and Sticky Grilled
    Chicken, 123
The Best Chicken Pasta
    Salad, 82
White Bean Chili, 20
Working Barn Stew, 78
Chili
Chili for a Crowd, 79
Téjas Chili, 79
White Bean Chili, 20
Chocolate
Buckeyes, 169
Chocolate Chip Banana
    Bread, 153
Chocolate Pie, 175
Cracker Candy, 169
Grandma's Chocolate
    Cake, 164
Grasshopper Pie, 174
Homemade Chocolate
    Ice Cream, 184
Irresistible Grace Cake, 165
Kim's Chocolate Chip
    Cookies, 170
Miss Bonnie's Cookies, 170
Sinful Chocolate Caramel
    Pie, 175
Southern White Chocolate
    Cake, 167

Superb and Simple
    Chocolate Mousse, 14
Clams
Linguine with White Clam
    Sauce, 139
Coconut
Cream of Coconut
    Cake, 166
Crunchy Granola, 65
Curry Dip, 14
Savory Green Beans with
    Coconut, 24
Southern White Chocolate
    Cake, 167
Coffee Cakes
Blueberry Coffee Cake, 58
Cranberry Sour Cream Coffee
    Cake, 59
Sophie's Coffee Cake, 60
Sour Cream Coffee
    Cake, 61
Cookies
Butter Cookies, 171
Date Nut Cookies, 171
Gingerbread Cookies, 172
Kim's Chocolate Chip
    Cookies, 170
Miss Bonnie's Cookies, 170
Molasses Ginger Cookies, 22
Wedding Cookies, 172
Cookies, Bar
Butterscotch Brownies, 173
German Coffee Bars, 173
Lemon Hazelnut Squares, 26
Raspberry Bars, 22
Corn
Amish Corn, 94
Gulf Shrimp Newspaper
    Dinner, 135
Low Georgia Boil, 136
Rustic Corn Dressing, 15
Corn Bread
Corn Light Bread, 156
Jalapeño Corn Bread, 157
Sour Cream Corn
    Bread, 156
Crab Meat
Crab Cakes, 39
Crab Swiss Bites, 39
Cranberry
Baked Brie with Cranberry
    Chutney, 12
Cranberry Oatmeal Nut
    Bread, 143
Cranberry Pork Roast, 118
Cranberry Salad, 17
Cranberry Salsa, 94
Cranberry Sour Cream Coffee
    Cake, 59

Cranberry Tea, 70
Hot Cranberry Mull, 67
Desserts. *See also* Cakes; Candy;
    Cheesecakes; Cookies;
    Ice Cream; Pies
Banana Pudding, 178
Butterscotch Crepes, 183
Fruit Pizza, 182
Summer Fruit Crisp, 181
Superb and Simple
    Chocolate Mousse, 14
Tiramisu, 180
Dips. *See also* Salsas
Bread Bowl Dip, 13
Cold Artichoke Dip, 31
Curry Dip, 14
Roasted Red Bell Pepper and
    Artichoke Dip, 30
Swiss Bacon Dip, 32
Vidalia Onion Dip, 31
Duck
Marinated Wild Duck
    Breasts, 130
Egg Dishes. *See also* Quiches;
    Soufflés
Breakfast Pizza, 48
Ham and Sunflower
    Frittata, 47
Serbian Eggs, 47
Feta
Feta and Sun-Dried Tomato
    Torta, 33
Feta Cheese Bread, 145
Feta Quiche Florentine, 50
Tomato and Feta Spaghetti
    Alfredo, 139
Fish. *See also* Salmon
Baked Fish Fillets, 131
Grilled Swordfish with Caper
    Sauce, 133
Grilled Tuna with Mango
    Salsa, 134
Frostings/Icings
Caramel Frosting, 161
Chocolate Frosting, 164
Cream Cheese Frosting, 162
White Chocolate Icing, 167
Fruit. *See also* Apple; Banana;
    Blueberry; Coconut;
    Cranberry; Lemon; Orange;
    Peach; Raspberry;
    Salads, Fruit; Salads,
    Gelatin; Strawberry
Brown's Breakfast, 65
Fruit Pizza, 182
Summer Fruit Crisp, 181
Gingerbread
Gingerbread Cookies, 172
Pumpkin Gingerbread, 155

189

Granola
Bread Machine Banana
Granola Bread, 146
Crunchy Granola, 65
Green Beans
Green Bean Salad with Basil
Vinaigrette, 21
Green Beans in Sweet
Vinaigrette, 91
Savory Green Beans with
Coconut, 24
Ground Beef
Authentic Swedish
Meatballs, 112
Chili for a Crowd, 79
Company Casserole, 113
Fourth of July Bean
Casserole, 92
Lasagna, 115
Spaghetti with Meat
Sauce, 114
Téjas Chili, 79
Ham
Baked Zucchini with
Parmesan and
Prosciutto, 103
Ham and Rolls, 19
Ham and Sunflower
Frittata, 47
West African Red Beans and
Rice, 121
Ice Cream
Homemade Chocolate
Ice Cream, 184
Homemade Vanilla
Ice Cream, 184
Lamb
Classic Rack of Lamb, 116
Marinated Lamb Chops, 117
Lemon
Lemon Hazelnut Squares, 26
Lemon Poppy Seed Bread, 154
Lemon Poppy Seed
Dressing, 86
Pasta with Lemon Cream
Sauce, 106
Menus
Art Show Opening Night, 11
Football and Tailgating
Party, 19
Holiday Dinner, 15
International Spring
Dinner, 23
Muffins
Applesauce Muffins, 62
Oatmeal Blueberry
Muffins, 63
Mushrooms
Mushroom Casserole, 96

Mushroom Pâté, 35
Roasted Wild Mushrooms, 95
Sautéed Fresh
Mushrooms, 95
Onions
Baked Sweet Onions, 97
Vidalia Onion Dip, 31
Orange
Curried Orange Rice, 104
Double-Orange Scones, 64
Honey Fruit Compote, 84
North African Orange
Salad, 23
Zesty Orange Rub for
Pork, 120
Pancakes
Featherlight Yogurt
Pancakes, 54
German Pancakes, 55
Honey Puffed Pancake, 56
Saturday Morning
Pancakes, 57
Swedish Pancakes, 57
Pasta
Lasagna, 115
Linguine with Chicken,
Sun-Dried Tomatoes and
Gorgonzola, 129
Linguine with White Clam
Sauce, 139
Pasta with Lemon Cream
Sauce, 106
Penne with Tomato Cream
Sauce, 106
Seaside Pasta, 138
Shrimp, Tomato and Herb
Pasta, 137
Spaghetti with Meat
Sauce, 114
Spinach Cannelloni, 140
Tomato and Feta Spaghetti
Alfredo, 139
Peach
Chilled Peach Soup, 74
Fresh Peach Pie, 176
Fruit Pizza, 182
Perfect Peachy Pork
Tenderloins, 119
Peppers
African Green Pepper and
Spinach, 24
Chinese Pepper Steak, 111
Jalapeño Corn Bread, 157
Roasted Red Bell Pepper and
Artichoke Dip, 30
Pies
Basic Pie Crust, 176
Buttermilk Pie, 174
Chocolate Pie, 175

Fresh Peach Pie, 176
Frozen Peanut Butter
Pie, 177
Grasshopper Pie, 174
Pecan Pie, 177
Pumpkin Chiffon Pie, 18
Sinful Chocolate Caramel
Pie, 175
Pizza
Breakfast Pizza, 48
Fruit Pizza, 182
Pork. See also Bacon; Ham;
Sausage
Barbecue Sandwiches, 21
Cranberry Pork Roast, 118
Favorite Party Pork
Tenderloins, 38
Grilled Pork with Salsa, 120
Honey Grilled Pork
Tenderloins, 119
Perfect Peachy Pork
Tenderloins, 119
Zesty Orange Rub for
Pork, 120
Potatoes
Baby Red Potatoes, 97
Breakfast Pizza, 48
Cheese Soup, 76
Gulf Shrimp Newspaper
Dinner, 135
Low Georgia Boil, 136
Parmesan Potatoes, 98
Potato Soup, 75
Potatoes Provençal, 98
Salmon, Leek and Potato
Gratin, 132
Scrumptious Potatoes, 100
Twice-Baked Potatoes, 99
Poultry. See Chicken; Turkey
Pumpkin
Pumpkin Chiffon Pie, 18
Pumpkin Gingerbread, 155
Quiches
Classic Colorado Quiche, 49
Feta Quiche Florentine, 50
Raspberry
Fruit Pizza, 182
Raspberry Bars, 22
Rice
Chicken with Fruited Wild
Rice, 124
Company Chicken
Casserole, 126
Curried Orange Rice, 104
French Onion Rice, 125
West African Red Beans and
Rice, 121
Salad Dressings
Balsamic Vinaigrette, 88

Cider Vinaigrette, 87
Fruit Salad Dressing, 83
Lemon Poppy Seed
    Dressing, 86
Raspberry Vinaigrette, 88
Red Wine Vinaigrette, 85
Salads, Fruit
Festive Fruit Salad, 83
Honey Fruit Compote, 84
North African Orange
    Salad, 23
Winter Fruit Salad with
    Lemon Poppy Seed
    Dressing, 86
Salads, Gelatin
Apricot Salad, 84
Cranberry Salad, 17
Salads, Main Dish
The Best Chicken Pasta
    Salad, 82
Salads, Pasta
The Best Chicken Pasta
    Salad, 82
Tri-Colored Vegetable Pasta
    Salad, 81
Salads, Vegetable
Asparagus Salad, 80
Broccoli and Bacon
    Salad, 80
Green Bean Salad with Basil
    Vinaigrette, 21
Green Salad with Raspberry
    Vinaigrette, 88
Romaine and Noodle
    Salad, 85
Spinach and Strawberry
    Salad, 87
Tri-Colored Vegetable Pasta
    Salad, 81
Salmon
Marinated Salmon, 133
Salmon, Leek and Potato
    Gratin, 132
Salsas
Black Bean Salsa, 29
Cranberry Salsa, 94
Mango Salsa, 134
Sandwiches
Barbecue Sandwiches, 21
Ham and Rolls, 19
Sausage
Breakfast Pizza, 48
Gulf Shrimp Newspaper
    Dinner, 135
Low Georgia Boil, 136
West African Red Beans and
    Rice, 121

Seafood. *See* Clams; Crab Meat;
    Fish; Shrimp
Shrimp
Barbecue Basil Shrimp, 40
Gulf Shrimp Newspaper
    Dinner, 135
Low Georgia Boil, 136
Seaside Pasta, 138
Shrimp Curry, 25
Shrimp Delight, 136
Shrimp, Tomato and Herb
    Pasta, 137
Thai Shrimp, 41
Side Dishes. *See also* Rice; Pasta
Nana's Cheese Grits, 53
Old-Fashioned Dressing, 105
Rustic Corn Dressing, 15
Smoothies
Berry Smoothie, 66
Brown's Breakfast, 65
Snacks
Cheese Wafers, 42
Crunchy Granola, 65
Pita Chips, 43
Soft Pretzels, 44
Soufflés
Basil Soufflé, 51
Cheese Soufflé, 52
Soups, Cold
Chilled Peach Soup, 74
Gazpacho, 73
Soups, Hot. *See also* Chili
Cheese Soup, 76
Chicken Artichoke Soup, 77
Homemade Chicken Noodle
    Soup, 77
Potato Soup, 75
Tomato Basil Soup, 76
Working Barn Stew, 78
Spinach
African Green Pepper and
    Spinach, 24
Bread Bowl Dip, 13
Classic Colorado Quiche, 49
Feta Quiche Florentine, 50
Layered Cheese Loaf, 34
Spinach and Strawberry
    Salad, 87
Spinach Artichoke
    Casserole, 101
Spinach Cabrinee, 101
Spinach Cannelloni, 140
Spinach Roll, 37
Spreads
Baked Brie with Cranberry
    Chutney, 12
Basil Tomato Tapenade, 32

Caviar Artichokes, 12
Feta and Sun-Dried Tomato
    Torta, 33
Layered Cheese Loaf, 34
Mushroom Pâté, 35
Squash
Baked Butternut Squash, 17
Low Georgia Boil, 136
Squash Casserole, 102
Strawberry
Berry Smoothie, 66
Festive Fruit Salad, 83
Spinach and Strawberry
    Salad, 87
Summer Fruit Crisp, 181
Sweet Potatoes
Holiday Sweet Potatoes, 100
Tarts
Summer Tomato Tart, 103
Tomatoes
Basil Tomato Tapenade, 32
Gazpacho, 73
Feta and Sun-Dried Tomato
    Torta, 33
Linguine with Chicken,
    Sun-Dried Tomatoes and
    Gorgonzola, 129
Penne with Tomato Cream
    Sauce, 106
Shrimp, Tomato and Herb
    Pasta, 137
Summer Tomato Tart, 103
Tomato and Feta Spaghetti
    Alfredo, 139
Tomato Basil Soup, 76
Turkey
Roast Turkey with Maple
    Herb Butter, 16
Vegetables. *See* Artichokes;
    Asparagus; Beans;
    Broccoli; Carrots; Corn;
    Green Beans; Mushrooms;
    Onions; Peppers;
    Potatoes; Pumpkin;
    Salads, Vegetable;
    Spinach; Squash;
    Sweet Potatoes; Tomatoes;
    Zucchini
Zucchini
Baked Zucchini with
    Parmesan and
    Prosciutto, 103

Colorful Cuisine

Fine Art and Cooking in Brentwood

YOUR ORDER	QUANTITY	TOTAL
Colorful Cuisine at $20.00 per book		$
Shipping and handling at $3.95 per book		$
TOTAL		$

Please make check payable to Brentwood Academy Parent Association.

Name

Street Address

City   State   Zip

Telephone Number

Email Address

To order by mail, send to:
Brentwood Academy Parent Association
Attention: Cookbook Committee
219 Granny White Pike
Brentwood, Tennessee 37027

Photocopies will be accepted.